Lives to Remember

BOOKS BY PETER UNDERWOOD

Lives to Remember

A case book on reincarnation

PETER UNDERWOOD
and LEONARD WILDER

With a Foreword by Dr Bernard Finch

ROBERT HALE · LONDON

© Peter Underwood and Leonard Wilder 1975
First published in Great Britain 1975

ISBN 0 7091 5224 8

Robert Hale & Company
Clerkenwell House
Clerkenwell Green
London EC1R 0HT

Filmset by Specialised Offset Services Ltd, Liverpool
and printed and bound in Great Britain by
Redwood Burn Limited, Trowbridge & Esher

Contents

This book is dedicated to the ladies:
Peggy Bailey, Joyce Underwood and
Joan Wilder, who have all, in different
ways, contributed so much

Acknowledgements

The authors wish to publicly record their appreciation and gratitude to Peggy and Bill Bailey for their splendid co-operation throughout this long investigation.

Peter Underwood also gratefully acknowledges the invaluable help received from and permission to quote granted by: Wing Commander H.H. Drummond, A.F.C, D.F.M: Dr A.R.G. Owen, M.A. and the Toronto Society for Psychical Research; the Reverend H.T. Robins, former Rector of Whimple; the Reverend H.G. Tucker, present Rector of Whimple; Professor Ian Stevenson and The American Society for Psychical Research; Ada J. Stewart and Peter Davies Limited, the publishers of her book *Falcon: The Autobiography of His Grace James the 4, King of Scots;* The Medical Society of London; The Royal Society of Medicine; Regimental Headquarters, Scots Guards; The British Society for Psychical Research; Westminister Reference Library; Farnham Public Library; and the British Museum.

"All the world's a stage,
And all the men and women merely players:
They have their exits and their entrances;
And one man in his time plays many parts . . ."

Shakespeare *As You Like It*

"When we compare the present
life of man with that time of which
we have no knowledge, it seems to
me like the swift flight of a lone
sparrow thro' the banqueting-hall
where you sit in the winter
months . . . This sparrow flies
swiftly in thro' one door of the
hall, and out thro'
another . . . Similarly, man
appears on earth for a little while,
but we know nothing of what
went on before this life, or what
follows."

The Venerable Bede (673–735)
The Ecclesiastical History of England

Foreword

From time immemorial Man has been concerned about survival after death. Many people now accept reincarnation as the only logical corollary to this belief, for if we do survive then our continued existence must have some kind of environment and millions of people consider that we exist again here on this earth. On the other hand, if you do not believe in survival no amount of argument will convince you of its truth.

There are some very striking and authentic case histories for which the most probable explanation would seem to be reincarnation. The use of hypnosis in an attempt to produce evidence of reincarnation is by no means new and has been tried by many investigators. These experiments certainly showed many interesting features for the subconscious mind does remember its past experiences and these can easily be brought out by hypnosis.

For a large section of the world's population reincarnation is not a theory but a practical code of ethics and is an essential part of their religions. There are also scattered references in the Bible, the Gospels and other religious books.

Of course, there are other hypotheses put forward by scientists to explain the phenomenon. There is the idea that memory traces are passed from mother to foetus via the placenta, the agent being protein molecules. Recent animal experiments have tended to support this theory.

Although it does not give all the answers this volume certainly gives food for thought.

B.E. Finch, M.R.C.S., L.R.C.P., D.C.H.
London NW11

Introduction

As a psychical researcher I have long been intrigued with evidence for such subjects as mediumistic and other alleged supernormal phenomena beyond consciousness: telepathy, clairvoyance, psycho-kinesis, precognition, divining, 'faith-healing', hauntings and reincarnation.

During the course of long investigation into these mysterious worlds I have organized and conducted world-wide experiments in telepathy and extra-sensory perception; attended and controlled seances and carried out tests with scores of mental and physical mediums; examined the evidence for spontaneous phenomena and spent hundreds of hours in allegedly haunted houses; but it was not until Leonard Wilder told me something of the remarkable story of his early experiments in apparently regressing Peggy Bailey that I had any close association with the strange phenomenon of reincarnation.

Some of those who accept reincarnation maintain that the inner self – or higher mind – of a person is immortal and may be repeatedly reborn in different individuals, thereby explaining the by no means rare impression during a first visit to a building, place or country of having been there before; of having known people one has never met before (in this life!); perhaps even explaining 'love at first sight'.

The idea of reincarnation is very old and in fact so old that it is impossible to tell where the idea originated. It is part of most of the ancient religions, certainly Hinduism and Buddism; the Greeks were familiar with reincarnation as evidenced by the writings of Pythagoras (who claimed to have been Euphorbus in a previous existence) and Plato; Caesar records its teaching in his somewhat unreliable *Commentaries* on the Gallic Wars; it was known to the early Church and was sufficiently popular to be officially pronounced as a heresy by the Council of Constantinople in the year 551.

Throughout history reincarnation has had its adherents,

through Swedenborg, David Hume, Goethe, Ibsen and
Maeterlinck to Arthur Conan Doyle and people like Professors
Ward and McTaggart of Camdridge. In our own time both
Lord Dowding and John Masefield are among the many
thoughtful and practical people who have told me that they
accepted the principle of reincarnation without question. I
recall too discussing the subject with Geraldine Cummins, one
of the world's best-known 'automatic' writers. She believed
that after the death of the physical body it was possible for a
number of inner selves to be united by one higher mind and to
depend on that higher mind for sustenance. She believed too
that the majority of people reincarnated not more than four
times, continuing to preserve fundamental individuality but
developing in character or 'spiritual' force until they felt that
life on earth was of no further value to them and that the final
inner self that had developed could best serve by contributing to
another person who was to be reincarnated. Thus a
reincarnated person might contain, in addition to his or her
own inner self, the remnants of a dozen or a thousand other
people; until that person too decided not to be reincarnated but
to contribute to another's reincarnation.

Shaw Desmond once talked to me about reincarnation. He
said he *knew* he had lived in Egypt some 3,500 years earlier;
and he told me in 1950 that he had recently met a man he had
killed in the arena in Rome 2,000 years before. I remember he
said that to understand the true meaning of sleep and what we
call dreaming is to understand something of our lives between
our incarnations, and his parting shot to me was: "The only
religion that matters is the religion that makes you unafraid of
death. That religion is reincarnation." He saw life on this
earth as a school where we learn the lessons that life has to
teach; that in the intervals of return we stayed in a world of
spirit where we were prepared for our next return to earth,
and that after our last reincarnation we left the earth for ever
to begin another type of existence in spirit, an infinitely higher
existence that lasted for ever.

One of the interesting theories on reincarnation is easily
explained by using radio as an analogy of what may take
place. It seems reasonable to suppose that the 'core' or 'centre'
of our beings (the 'mind' or 'soul' if you like, or the 'psi-

component') leaves the body at the moment of physical death in much the same way as a radio signal leaves a transmitter and it is suggested that this 'signal' carries with it the 'personality data' of the individual concerned and that this is in turn picked up by a suitable 'receiver' – perhaps almost immediately, perhaps not for a long time. The right receiver will probably be the developing brain of an unborn child and again on a par with radio signals, it may be that when the psi-component leaves one dead body it can only 'tune in' on a developing brain that is uniquely suited to receive it. It is an attractive theory from a number of viewpoints, and one that has found favour with some scientists including agnostic Sir Julian Huxley who has intimated that he can see nothing against such a theory.

As with so many aspects of psychical research there are many theories but few facts.

Of course there have been many equally thoughtful and interested people who have studied the subject and arrived at the conclusion that they cannot accept the possibility of reincarnation. Andrew Jackson Davis, the American clairvoyant and prophet, used to refer to the idea as "a magnificent mansion built on sand", while Daniel Dunglas Home, possibly the most famous of all physical mediums, once referred, somewhat inaccurately, to the fact that in the field of reincarnation he had "had the pleasure of meeting at least twelve Marie Antoinettes, six or seven Marys of Scotland, a whole host of Louis and other kings, about twenty Great Alexanders, but never a plain John Smith..." He would certainly have been intrigued by the Peggy Bailey story.

Over the years I have been considerably interested in curious experiences where reincarnation would appear to be the most obvious explanation and conclusion; sufficiently interested in fact to carry out a certain amount of research to establish the authenticity of the reported circumstances.

In 1955, for example, I tried, unsuccessfully, to locate a Canadian naval officer who came to England in the 1930s when he took up duties at Chatham and obtained living accommodation for himself, his wife and their seven-year-old daughter at nearby Rochester, quite close in fact to the ruined

Norman castle. Most Sundays, so ran the report, the young family would stroll round the delightful Medway town, but one day it was decided that they would visit the impressive castle ruins that are believed to date from about the year 1100.

As they walked towards the castle the little girl looked up at her mother and asked whether they had always lived in the "little apartment?" Without much attention being given to the matter the child was told that of course they had not always lived where they now were; she knew full well that they came from Ottawa. But she didn't mean that, the little girl insisted, "I mean long, long ago when we lived up there" – and she pointed to a window high up in the castle walls.

Admonitions were ineffective in quietening her, and the child, her eyes bright and her voice eager with sincerity, insisted that she and her parents had indeed once lived in a big room at the castle, a room where there was a lot of straw on the floor, no glass in the windows and where it was bitterly cold at night.

Mother and father looked at one another. How did the child know that the Normans used straw to cover the floors of their rooms? Some picture book probably . . . They questioned her more closely and without effort or hesitation she described in detail not only the room she said she had lived in with a stairway in the corner, but also her friend, a little boy who lived in a room below; and then she began to minutely describe the clothes that she and the boy had worn in those days.

More than a little puzzled by what seemed to be a kind of day-dreaming, the family passed into the precincts of the castle and immediately the child pointed to a spiral stairway leading to one of the surviving castle turrets. "There are the stairs to our room!" she exclaimed, "and that's where a big fire was kept burning all winter, but it was still cold sometimes."

When they reached the first floor the child claimed that they were in the room where she used to play with her little friend, Stephen, a boy with fair hair; and on the second floor she broke away from her parents and ran towards a corner exclaiming, "Look – here was where I slept, and you and daddy slept there . . ."

Next day the naval officer called at the local library and discovered that his young daughter's description of the clothing worn by herself and her little friend tallied to the smallest detail with costumes worn by children in the middle of the twelfth century. Whatever the explanation, the child, usually unimaginative and rather shy, always seemed to be completely at home and familiar with every part of Rochester Castle; as it had been 900 years before.

When, in 1972, I was researching some of the ghost stories associated with the Tower of London, I discovered that a nine-year-old girl from the north of England, visiting London for the first time in her life, related a fact not known to her parents or, it seems, to anyone else present.

While a guide was reciting a list of execution victims on Tower Green, the name of Anne Boleyn was included as one of those who had been beheaded by the headsman's axe and at once the little girl whispered to her mother: "They didn't chop her head off with an axe. They did it with a sword." Afterwards, as they left the Tower, she described in detail to her astonished parents the scene in 1536 when a compassionate executioner removed his shoes so that he could approach her without notice, crept behind the queen and killed her with his sword.

In fact this is exactly what happened although most authorities concur with *Chamber's Encyclopaedia* which states: "Anne submitted her slim neck to the headsman's axe'. The *Encyclopaedia Britannica* however refers to the queen's head "being struck off with a sword by the executioner of Calais, being brought to England for the purpose."

I ascertained that the girl had no particular interest in history; she had read no detailed life of Anne, or of Henry VIII, nor had she seen any television programme of the period or studied the period at school. She was quite ignorant of other elementary facts of the time and it did seem that in some mysterious way she had obtained this particular fact from an unknown and inexplicable source. The girl herself could offer no explanation; she said she just knew all about it and felt that she had been there at the time.

These and other experiences, seemingly inexplicable and always interesting, are part and parcel of a psychical

researcher's occasional postbag, but when Leonard Wilder
first related to me something of the quite fascinating story of
Peggy Bailey I was particularly grateful because here, I felt,
for the first time was the opportunity to study at firsthand
work by an acknowledged hypnotist in the field of age
regression.

One of the first aspects of the apparent regressions under
hypnosis of Peggy Bailey that Leonard Wilder discussed with
me was the striking and emphatic deep breathing that nearly
always preceded regression to a different period of time and I
immediately recalled that much stertorous breathing is often
noticed in spiritualist mediums during trance; it was
particularly remarked upon in the mediumship of the late Mrs
Osborn Leonard. While reposing pleasantly (after the very
deep breathing) the medium seemed to act as a human
telephone operator in touch with the world beyond . . .

The exploration and experimentation of such a case as
Leonard Wilder outlined to me could not be less than
interesting and might well be valuable and far-reaching; but
before attempting any assessments, conclusions or exploring
possible explanations – including the formidable obstacle of
unconscious 'role-taking' – let us hear Leonard Wilder's own
account of the history of Peggy Bailey and his experiments in
hypnotism with her.

Peter Underwood

The Savage Club
St James's Street
London SW1

1
The Prelude

1957 was a remarkable year for me. For in that year two apparently unrelated events occurred without which this book would never have been written. In the summer of that year I completed a course on hypnosis at the Royal Society of Medicine. Later in the year, in December, I obtained my private pilot's licence.

If you were to consider the condition under which you had met your husband or your wife, or found yourself in any situation which had greatly affected your life, it was possibly just a very chance event which had led up to the meeting. It was, in fact, a casual remark by a professional colleague of mine that prompted me to take a course on hypnosis.

The reason for my becoming a pilot was very much by chance. For some years after I qualified as a dental surgeon I had been a member of Guy's Hospital motoring club. Despite having participated in a number of minor rallies I had never won or even come near to winning. In the autumn rally of October 1956, to my surprise and delight, I and my two navigators arrived at the final check-point nearly half an hour ahead of any other car. The check-point was a flying club in Hertfordshire. Enjoying the distinction and satisfaction of being first, we rested in the car and waited for the other competitors to arrive. I soon found myself being fascinated by the small, light aircraft, that raced across the grass, bounced awkwardly a few times and then rose gracefully into the freedom of the air. I had, at last, won a rally. I could never do better than come first again. That challenge had been met. I decided to retire from motor-car rallies and invest the new-found time in learning to fly.

My two colleagues, caught by my enthusiasm, agreed to do the same. As we returned to our homes, each the proud owner of a silver cup, we decided to join the Elstree Flying Club and start flying lessons. Whatever their reasons were, my friends stayed on terra firma while I, alone, ventured into the air. After about forty hours' tuition I found myself as a qualified pilot on 31 December 1957. And this is where my experiences as a hypnotist and as a pilot started to converge.

My early use of hypnosis was confined, quite naturally, to its application in dentistry. I used it to allay fear and apprehension in nervous patients and, in suitable subjects, to produce full surgical anaesthesia, so that the extraction of teeth and the performance of minor oral surgery could be carried out without any recourse to conventional local or general anaesthetics. It still seems quite incredible to me that just through the power of suggestion, albeit carried out in a very special way, complete numbness of the teeth and jaws can be achieved.

During these early days I became more and more interested in the work of some researchers in the field of age regression under hypnosis. In order to be able to satisfactorily regress a subject, it is necessary for the hypnotist to produce in him a state of deep trance. Although it is not easy to classify the various states of trance, most hypnotists agree that three phases can be defined. The first is light trance, where the subject is relaxed with eyes closed and capable of responding to such suggestions as a feeling of extreme lightness in an arm. To the subject's surprise he or she finds the arm rising up into the air without any apparent conscious motivation. In medium trance, the subject will respond to post-hypnotic suggestions. That is, the suggestion is made during trance that he will carry out a specific act in the normal, waking state, after the removal of hypnosis. For example, I might state to a subject that "Ten minutes after I wake you up, you will feel very thirsty and ask for a drink of water." A subject who experiences a compulsion to have a drink just as suggested is said to be capable of producing medium trance. Various other phenomena are observable under the categories of light and medium trance, but I will not elaborate on these as our main interest at this point is in the next and most interesting level of trance. That is, the condition of deep hypnosis.

For the dentist and surgeon this state is of particular value as it is here that surgical procedures can be performed. I could hardly believe what I was doing when I first started to extract teeth in this way. No local injection, no anaesthetist, but instead a relaxed, conscious and almost indifferent patient sitting there calmly in the dental chair. I must confess to having been far more concerned than my patient. I have to repeat my earlier sentiment that it really is quite remarkable what the power of suggestion can do.

I now come to what, to me, is the most exciting of all phenomena producible under deep trance hypnosis. That is, the ability of the hypnotist to take certain deep trance subjects back in time. Here, the subject will regress to specific events in his lifetime and not just remember but actually relive these events. The subject is able to converse quite freely with the hypnotist, in this state, and describe in detail what is happening. The past becomes the present. Events long forgotten in conscious life are brought up from the deep depths of the subconscious. Provided the hypnotist tells his subject that at all times he, the hypnotist, will be understood in English (or the national language of the hypnotist and subject), then the subject can be regressed to quite early infancy.

Since this is not a textbook on hypnotism I will omit details of hypnosis technique. But I have to mention here a word of caution. Hypnotism, like any specialized procedure, should only ever be performed by a competent and qualified person. Otherwise, certain unexpected and unpleasant situations could arise in inexperienced hands. To return to my remark about being understood in English. This is a paramount precaution. It is possible that the subject quite unknown to the hypnotist, was born in a foreign country and had come to this country as a small child. Having then been completely educated here there would, of course, be no trace of a foreign accent. Few people would, indeed, know of the subject's national origin. Imagine then if a hypnotist, completely unaware of the situation, had said to such a person in a deep trance, "You will go back to your fourth birthday and tell me all about it." Had the subject come to this country at the age of five from for example, Hungary, then unless the hypnotist could speak Hungarian all further communication between them would be lost. Here would be a situation where a small

Hungarian child could not converse with or understand his English hypnotist. There are methods of extricating oneself from this easily avoidable situation but no hypnotist should allow such a position to arise.

By telling the subject that "You will at all times understand me in English," the subject can always be progressed from the regressed state and brought back again to the present. The hypnotist might not be able to understand the language spoken by his regressed subject. This is unfortunate, but certainly not serious. At least he, the hypnotist, is being understood and that is what matters. I once had a very charming lady whom I regressed to the age of three, when to my amazement she started to sing a nursery rhyme in Russian, my knowledge of which is virtually non-existent. Fortunately, I had taken the above precaution. Which stresses my point.

Something that occurs quite spontaneously with regressable deep trance subjects is what is known as post hypnotic amnesia. That is, having been brought back again from the past to the present and awakened, the subject has no memory whatever of having been regressed. To him or her the passage of time is not recognized. Two hours in deep trance could seem more like five or ten minutes of sleep. I like to see the look of astonishment in a subject's face when, after a couple of hours in deep trance, he notices the time and can hardly believe what has happened.

To the psychiatrist who practises hypno-therapy, age regression can be a valuable tool. Used correctly, past traumatic experiences (now repressed by the patient and possibly the initiating cause of a neurosis) can be discovered, analysed and evaluated. If considered prudent by the physician, such knowledge could assist in devising methods of treatment. I believe that today the use of regression in psychiatry is only resorted to in special cases. However, this is not my field of investigation.

The interesting speculation at this point is that, if a deep trance hypnosis subject can relive his earlier life's experiences right down to the moment of birth, then, provided this is an authentic fact, perhaps he can be regressed to a previous lifetime to relive once again the memories stored away in his psychic memory. This concept is not new and other hypnotists have produced phenomena which would appear to verify this procedure. But I had not yet in the early days of 1958 investigated the field of reincarnation, or what appeared to be the case for reincarnation. It was an experience I had to try for myself. I studied the technique and hoped to find a suitable subject for investigation.

While I was developing as a hypnotist I spent what leisure I had enjoying the freedom of the air. My wife Joan, who at that time was my fiancée, would spend every weekend with me exploring the skies over England and then with increasing confidence venturing across the English Channel to France, the Continent and the Channel Isles. In those days we did not have the sophisticated radio aids enjoyed today. Flying was by 'dead reckoning' and a converted one-inch Ordnance Survey map. As with my hypnosis, flying was an adventure.

Joan and I became good friends with the chief flying instructor of Elstree Flying Club and his wife, Bill and Peggy Bailey. It was Bill who had played a major part in teaching me to fly, and as an examiner for the private pilot's licence had eventually decided that I could be allowed to fly passengers as a qualified pilot. At about this time the Bailey's were involved in a minor car accident. As a result, Peggy was thrown forward on to the instrument panel and fractured her nose. This healed uneventfully but left her with an understandable fear of being driven in a car. She would become terrified if her husband drove faster than twenty miles an hour, which can have its problems on a long journey. This created such limitations to their transport as to become a considerable problem.

One evening when we had all been having coffee together Peggy turned to me and said, "Leonard, can't you hypnotize Bill so that he is not annoyed with me when I get nervous in the car?" Before I could answer, Bill interjected, "Wouldn't it be better if you could cure Peggy's fear of motoring, under hypnosis?" I had never before tried anything like this and felt that it should be managed by a specialist in this field. These were early days for me in the realms of hypnotism. I had only one year's experience so far and that (in 1958) had been exclusively confined to dental patients. I explained this to

them. Peggy assured me that she had confidence in me and
that on no account would she "go to a stranger who didn't
understand her". She said she "felt rather silly about the
whole thing and please, Leonard, do try this hypnotism." I
felt I really should have an attempt. Joan urged me to as well.
I invited Peggy on to the couch which I used specifically for
hypnosis. Joan and Bill sat quietly behind me. Peggy had
never been hypnotized before.

Using a traditional technique, I very quickly put her into
light trance. I conducted a few simple tests and then within
just a few minutes I had her in what appeared to be a state of
medium trance. I suggested that when I woke her up her feet
would feel warm and she would remove her shoes and that one
minute after that she would ask for another cup of coffee. I
decided at that stage to bring her out of trance and see just
how deep she had really gone. I did so. Peggy opened her eyes,
rubbed them and sat up.

"I think I must have dozed off for a minute," she yawned.
She had actually been under hypnosis nearly fifteen minutes.
"It's so comfortable on this couch. I'm ready when you are,
Leonard," she said.

"Ready for what?" I asked.

"Ready for you to start the hypnosis," she said with
surprise, "or have you changed your mind?"

Spontaneous post-hypnotic amnesia! She had remembered
nothing at all! She had been much deeper than I realized.
Here was an excellent subject who had produced deep trance
in just a few minutes of her very first session. I had a quick
glance at Joan and Bill, who sat impassively in their chairs.

"Of course not, Peggy," I quickly reassured her, "I'm ready
to start when you are."

Peggy hesitated for a moment. "Do you mind if I remove
my shoes first?" she asked. "My feet are feeling hot this
evening."

I gave my assent. "Shall we start then, Peggy?" I went on.

"If there's any more coffee left in the pot could I have
another quick cuppa first?" Peggy asked. "I don't know why,
but I feel so thirsty this evening." Joan poured out a cup of
coffee and handed it to Peggy.

May I briefly point out at this stage that what was

happening was neither new, unique nor special to hypnosis. It was, however, to become in due course a new, unique and special experience for all of us in that room.

Peggy finished her coffee and settled comfortably on the couch. Within moments, this time, I had induced in her a state of very deep trance. As I watched her lying there almost motionless, breathing slowly and rhythmically, I realized that here was good, potential material for regression. I filed the idea away in my mind. Perhaps one day . . .

I explained to Peggy that the reason she was still afraid of being driven by her husband was her persistent association with Bill and the accident and that the chance of another accident was remote. In future, I said, her attitude to car travelling would become quite normal. I told her that she would gradually lose her fears so that within a short time she would be completely cured of her phobia. I had another quick look at Bill, who nodded his approval at what I had said. I hoped I had gone about it the right way. Feeling just a little anxious, I woke Peggy up. It took us all a little time to convince her that she really had been hypnotized. Reference to her wristwatch and the confirmation of the passage of time soon convinced her. "It just doesn't seem possible," she commented. "I don't feel as though I've been under at all." I requested that she should come to see me again in a week's time in order to assess what progress she had made and to have another session in order to strengthen the effect of the hypnosis. The Baileys left.

The journey to their home at Elstree would normally take about twenty minutes. Driving slowly one would expect a time of about thirty minutes. Fifteen minutes after they left the telephone rang. Imagine my surprise when I heard Bill's voice. For a moment I thought that perhaps something unpleasant had happened on their way and that he was not telephoning from home. I was quickly reassured.

"Leonard," he shouted excitedly through the telephone, "you've done it. You've cured Peggy! I was driving at twenty miles an hour and decided to cautiously put it up to thirty. I did so and held the speed there. Suddenly Peggy turned to me and said 'What's wrong with the car? Won't it go any faster or are you afraid of a little speed?' When I reminded her how nervous she was of driving, she protested and said, 'That was only after the accident. Not now. Come on Bill, get your foot down!'''

As planned, Bill and Peggy returned to see me the following week. Bill reported that Peggy was absolutely normal in her sentiments to car travel. All her previous fears had disappeared. Peggy in turn had made no mention of the incident at all during the week. My fiancée, who by now was naturally fascinated by these events, was also present. Without too many preliminaries I soon had Peggy in a state of deep trance. Once again I reiterated the 'treatment of the previous week. Once again Peggy had complete post-hypnotic amnesia. However, this time she accepted without much persuasion that she had been in trance and had received more hypnosis for her car nerves. Despite the obvious cure, I thought it prudent to give her yet another 'booster dose' the following week just to consolidate. Once again, a week later, the Baileys arrived and within a few minutes I had administered to Peggy what must now be the final session in the cure of her motoring phobia. She really was completely cured. They had been on the premises barely fifteen minutes and the evening was still very young . . .

Regression! And I thrilled as the thought came to me. I can still feel to this day the excitement at the prospect of personally venturing into this field. It was the same sense of anticipation, tinged with a little fear, that I had felt as I sat in a small, throbbing aeroplane at the end of the runway just before my first solo flight. The conditions were similar. I was about to venture alone into a new dimension and having crossed the threshold only I had control of the situation. Only I could bring back the flying machine or the 'time machine'. It was Bill Bailey who the previous year had authorized my first solo flight. And so once again I turned to Bill Bailey to authorize a 'flight into the past'.

Bill knew nothing about age regression under hypnosis. I spent a little time explaining the concepts to him. I told him that although I had studied and understood the technique this would be my first experiment. I hastily reassured him that I would take all necessary precautions and that in no way would Peggy suffer any harm, either physically or psychically.

Suddenly I felt a surge of confidence and I knew that this was
the right moment to start. During all this time Peggy lay
peacefully on the couch, neither hearing what we were saying
nor caring. Bill reflected for a moment and then gave me his
full approval. "Okay, Leonard, go ahead," he said.

2
The First Regression

Joan leaned forward in her chair and tapped me on the shoulder. "Switch on your tape-recorder," she advised. In two minutes the machine was ready and switched on to record. I turned to Peggy still lying quietly on the couch and addressed myself directly to her.

"Are you quite comfortable?" I asked.

"Yes, thank you," she replied in a somewhat subdued voice.

"I want you to go back in time. I want you to go back in time to the morning of your wedding day to Bill. I want you to go back in time to the morning of your wedding day to Bill. Back in time. It is now the morning of your wedding day. The morning of your wedding day." I decided to repeat the instructions so as to allow Peggy a little more time to locate and adjust to that time in her past that I had indicated.

"What is the date?" I continued.

"July 1st, 1950," she answered. Peggy had started to regress!

"And what is your name?"

"Margaret Frances Beeching."

"And what's happening today?"

"I'm going to be married today."

"To whom?"

"To William Henry Bailey."

"And where are you living at the moment?"

"2 Willow Close, Elm Park, Hornchurch."

"And where are you going to live after you are married to William?"

"We don't know yet. We haven't found anywhere."

"I see. What sort of day is it today?"

"It's a lovely day, sun shining and the birds are singing."

"What does William do? What is his work?"

"He's an engineer."

"He's done a lot of flying, hasn't he?"

"Yes, during the war."

"He was a pilot, was he?"

"Yes."

"Right. I want you to go back in time and you're getting younger and younger. You're getting younger and younger and you're going back now to your thirteenth birthday. You are thirteen years old today. This is your thirteenth birthday. How old are you today?" Having stated the age to which I wanted her to regress, I asked her how old she was to verify the accuracy of the regression.

"I'm thirteen."

"And what is your name?"

"Margaret Frances Beeching, but I'm called Peggy."

I sensed that she was becoming more relaxed. Possibly, the start of the regression had produced a little nervousness. Her voice was more assured and she had now offered me a little gratuitous information and a hint of informality.

"You're called Peggy? Well, I'm going to call you Peggy."

"Yes."

"And where do you live, Peggy?"

"65 Jackson's Lane, Romford."

"And do you go to school?"

"Yes."

"What school?"

"London Road."

"Do you like it?"

"Yes."

"Good. Now Peggy, I want you to go back in time and you're getting younger and younger, younger and younger, and today is your sixth birthday. Today you are six. How old are you?"

"I'm six." Her voice had become noticeably younger.

"And what is the date, do you know?"

"Yes, it's the 1st of December."

"And what is the year? Do you know?"

"Ooh, I don't count very well."

"Don't you count very well?"

"No."

"What year were you born? Do you know?"

"Yes, 1921."

"So this will be 1927, won't it?"

"Yes."

"Very good. Are you going to have a party?"

"Some children."

"Who's coming?"

"Ooh, the little boy downstairs and I don't think his brother can come because he's always in bed. He's a poor sick little boy."

"I am sorry. Right Peggy, I want you to go back in time and you're getting younger and younger . . . going back . . . going back . . ." (Here Peggy took a deep, deep breath. An obstetrician friend of mine who at a later date listened to the recording said it reminded him of the first breath of a newborn baby. Peggy and many other subjects that I subsequently regressed repeated this deep breath nearly each time they were sent to a different time stage. It is interesting to note that it did not always occur, even with Peggy Bailey.) ". . . going back to your third birthday. Today you are three. Today is your third birthday, Peggy. How old are you, dear?"

"I'm Thwee." (The intonation of a child.)

"How old?"

"Thwee."

"And what is your name?"

"Peg-gy."

"Peggy what?"

"Peggy Beaching." (A suggestion of childish uncertainty.)

"And have you any brothers and sisters, dear?"

"Yes, John."

"And anyone else?"

"No, only John."

"Is he older than you or younger?"

"Oh he's a little boy."

"Is he?"

"M-m-m."

"And you don't go to school yet, do you?"

"No."

"You don't."

"But I know some letters." (I was intrigued by her sudden offer of friendship and an attempt to develop the conversation.)

"Do you? What letters do you know?"

"A . . . B . . . m,m,m . . . D" (Somewhat unsure.)

"That's very good."

"I don't think I know any more."

"Very good."

As it was suddenly offered, so her co-operation was suddenly withdrawn, just like a small child who has been questioned too much and has become fatigued.

I decided to rest her for a moment while I recovered from this remarkable experience. As I said earlier on, age regression of a hypnotized person in a deep trance is not new. But this was my adventure, or rather our adventure, and I had to consider the next move. Should I bring her back to the present time and perhaps attempt further investigations at another session? Or should I continue while the opportunity presented itself? My curiosity was very great. The temptation to attempt a regression back into a past life of Peggy Bailey was overwhelming. Would she respond? Was she too tired? Or perhaps the leap back from the age of three was just the right point from which to take her. She was very peaceful on the couch. Outwardly, she was my friend, Peggy Bailey, in her mid-thirties and married to Bill Bailey, the chief flying instructor of Elstree Flying Club. Yet she had just told me, indeed had actually been, a little girl called Peggy Beeching, aged "thwee", living with her family in Romford, Essex. I hesitated for a moment, switched off the tape recorder and weighed up the situation.

And it is at this point of the book that I must reflect and prepare for the ensuing pages. Although it may be a little frustrating to have an interlude from the story of Peggy Bailey, it will add greater interest to the rest of the book if certain facts are considered and illustrated with examples. For in the event of my further regressing Peggy Bailey and should this produce positive results, what would be the implications? Certainly the possibility of reincarnation! There may well be other explanations. I did not consider myself at that time qualified to evaluate such facts. However, if one is going to even consider the possibility of reincarnation then the existence of a psyche, soul, spirit, astral body, etheric body – call it what you will – must be presupposed.

For some years I had been interested in the experiences of

people who have come very near to death as the result of an
accident, yet have survived to tell of their experiences. I would
like to relate a few of these. As I do so an interesting aspect
will emerge. Although the incidents are quite different, a basic
experience will readily be seen to be common to them all.

Example 1: Mrs Bateman

Some years ago a lady came to my dental practice as a new
patient. She required the removal of a tooth, but asked me not
to use a general anaesthetic as she said she had had a strange
experience the last time she had received inhalation
anaesthesia in the dental chair. When I questioned her
further, I heard the following story. I quote her words.

"I had been to this dentist before and knew him well but this
was the first time it had been necessary for him to extract one
of my teeth. I was in good health apart from my painful tooth.
The dentist's partner came in from the next room. He placed
the nose-piece of his gas machine over my nose and asked me
to breathe deeply in and out. As I drifted away I noticed the
nurse standing on the left of the chair. The dentist was waiting
at my right side. The next thing I knew was that I seemed to
be standing at the foot of the chair, facing it. I could see myself
sitting there, slumped slightly to one side. Both dentists were
slapping my face, while the nurse was loosening my clothing. I
felt perfectly fit, watching everything from the other side of the
room. No one seemed to be aware of my presence there. They
were too busy, obviously trying to resuscitate my physical
body.

"'She's in a bad way,' I heard the dentist say. 'Call her
doctor, quickly!' The nurse anxiously inspected my record
card and dialled a number.

"'At the golf club!' She exclaimed when the telephone was
answered.

"'Please phone him there. It's extremely urgent.'

"The next thing I knew was that I found myself at the
doctor's golf club and to my amazement saw him hurrying out
of the club house. He rushed to his car and drove off furiously
in the direction of the dentist's practice. The journey was
quite short and soon he was bounding up to the first floor
where the surgery was. He still had on his golfing jacket and

wore a cloth cap. He threw the cap on to a chair in the entrance hall and dashed into the room. I followed him in and watched in a detached sort of way while he gave my physical body an injection and massaged my chest. Suddenly, I found myself being drawn back into my body. I felt reluctant to go. Then I woke up in the dental chair feeling awful and with a splitting headache.

"When I had recovered somewhat, and this was not until after some time, I told them of my experience. They didn't believe me of course and I don't blame them. It did sound an odd sort of story. But when I remembered the doctor tossing his cap on to the chair in the hall they had another think. I also told him what he didn't know. He had been in such a rush that the cap had slid off the chair and was now on the floor beside it. They all rushed out of the surgery. I shall never forget the amazed looks on their faces when they came back. The cap was exactly where I had told them . . . on the floor!"

Example 2: Philip Saville

A renowned television and film director was taken skin-diving by a friend. He had never participated in the sport before and he was warned not to venture too deep. He donned his aqualung and went down. After a little while he found himself in difficulties with a blockage in his air supply. He struggled and then found himself floating out of his body and looking down on himself, lying helpless on the seabed. Almost immediately his friend dragged him to the surface, pulled him into the boat, snatched off his mask and applied artificial respiration. Reluctantly, he found himself going back into his body again and regained consciousness to find himself on dry land.

Example 3: Mr Simons

A gentleman I met only once told me a story about himself that has left me with a vivid impression to this day. His right arm had been amputated at the shoulder. During conversation I referred to my interest in what appeared to be an exteriorization, whereupon he related the following story. At the age of seventeen he had become the proud owner of a motorcycle. One day, when travelling too fast, he had skidded on a slippery road and had felt his machine falling from beneath him. The next thing he knew was that he was standing in the street and a group of people were bending over something or someone in the road. "What a ghastly mess!" he heard someone say. He peered over the crowd and to his utter amazement saw someone who closely resembled himself lying very still in the road. The clothes were torn and bathed in blood. He noticed that the right arm was badly twisted and smashed. At seventeen he had never given psychic matters even a fleeting thought and so he stood there in a state of confusion. An ambulance arrived and the men carried his injured double inside. And then he identified the bent and buckled remains of his motorcycle lying in the road several yards away. Then it seemed as if some unseen force was pushing and pulling him in the direction of the retreating ambulance and he felt himself rushing uncontrollably through the air at great speed. The next thing he knew he was waking up in a hospital bed with a very painful right shoulder.

Example 4: Howard Livens

During World War I an army captain was engaged on work with experimental explosives. One day, while testing a device in the middle of a field, he saw a flash, heard a violent bang and found himself tumbling through the air. To his surprise instead of crashing heavily to the ground his wild gyrations were replaced by a gentle, almost pleasant, floating sensation and he then found himself, apparently quite intact and unharmed by the explosion, standing at the edge of the field. Several people were shouting and running wildly to the middle of the field where his device had blown up. He ran after them calling and trying to attract their attention. No one took any notice of him. As he approached the group that had now formed, one of the officers said, "Poor old Howard, it looks as though he's nearly had it." He then caught sight of 'himself' lying unconscious on the grass. The shock of this discovery was so great that it jerked him back into his body and he seemed to black out. Several hours later he regained consciousness in a military hospital and in due course made an uneventful recovery.

I could relate a great number of similar stories. A sudden trauma and impending death, producing what would appear to be evidence of detachment of the psyche or second body. Such apparent out-of-the-body experiences are not confined exclusively to cases where physical trauma has taken place. There are many recorded cases where this has occurred spontaneously. Jeremy Lloyd, the actor-writer, was on the verge of dropping off to sleep in bed one evening when he suddenly felt as though he were being detached from his body and floating up out of himself. He was able to see right through a misty outline of his legs. Knowing the subject well, he quickly recognized the phenomenon that was starting to happen. He wondered if it were possible to visit a friend of his just by willing himself to do so. Almost in a flash he found himself in his friend's drawing-room, a room he knew well. He was able to move about quite freely and managed to recognize several objects. He noticed what he described as a thick, tough band of elastic material, attached to himself and stretching away into the distance. This appeared to have caught against a shiny metallic object that he could not identify, standing on the end of the piano. He pulled the elastic cord in order to free it. Suddenly he felt a jerk, followed by a rushing sensation. He woke up in bed in his own home. He immediately telephoned his friend and asked what the strange, new metallic object was on the end of the grand piano. "I bought a silver candlestick today," came the reply, "and liked it so much that I stood it on the end of the piano. But you haven't been here for a few days, so how do you know?. . . !"

It is not my role within the compass of this book to elaborate on the interpretation of these incidents. This I entrust entirely to Peter Underwood. My contribution at this stage is to record the facts and to leave evaluation open for hypothesis. However, having at least established the possibility of the existence of a psyche, the road along which I might be able to regress Peggy Bailey to a previous life or lives was now open. The assessment of this with other explanations rests with the psychic researcher.

3
Sally Fraser

To return again to Peggy Bailey, resting in deep hypnosis on the couch in my room in the presence of myself, my fiancée, and Peggy's husband, Bill. Remember that she had just been regressed from the adult woman to the child of three. I was ready to produce a phenomenon that may well take her on a great leap back into the past, ready to unravel the hidden stories that were deep in her psychic memory. Past joys, tragedies, hopes, failures, aspirations, the emotions of which could be stored away like the electro-magnetic impulses recorded on a plastic tape and ready to be released, replayed, revealed and relived in response to the right signal.

I checked that the record button of my tape-recorder was back in the 'on' position and addressed myself again to Peggy. As I felt my pulse racing I took a breath and said:

"Right. Now I want you to go back in time. I want you to go back in time a long, long, way . . . going back in time. You are going back in time to a time before you were born what you are now. You are going back in time to a time [she took a deep breath] before you were born what you are now . . . when you were some other person on this earth . . . to a time when you were someone else on this earth. You may have to go back a long, long time, but you're going back, you're going back . . . back, back, back in time . . . and now you're someone on this earth . . . someone on this earth. Who are you?" A few seconds' silence.

"I'm Sally!"

"Sally? Hello Sally. Sally what?"

"Sally Fraser . . . sir." (I noticed a slight roll to the 'r's.)

"And what is the date, Sally Fraser?"

"It's . . . oh! it's 1733." (There was a definite West Country accent.)

"Is it?" (Prepared though I was, I was taken by surprise.)

"Yes sir."

"Where do you live?"

"On a farm."

"Where is the farm, Sally?"

"It's in Devon." (She pronounced it *Davon.*)

"In . . .?"

"In Devon."

"And are there any rivers or any lakes near you or anything?"

"Oh yes, there's a river."

"Which river?"

"It's the River Exe."

"Axe or Exe?"

"Exe." (It sounded like either.)

"I see. How do you spell it?"

"E . . x . . e."

"I see; and have you any brothers or sisters?"

"Yes, just one."

"Brother or sister?"

"A brother."

"What's his name?"

"Tom." (She pronounced it *Tarm.*)

"And how old are you, Sally?"

"Oh, I'm seventeen."

"How old's Tom?"

"Tom's ten."

"I see; and what do you do during the day? What do you do?"

"Oh, I help my mother [pronounced *Mither*] on the farm."

"What sort of a farm have you got?"

"Well . . . just a farm . . . with cows, pigs and the horses."

"How about your father, what does he do?"

"Well, he's the farmer. He owns the farm."

"How about market-day? Do you have a market-day ever?"

"Oh yes, in Exeter."

"How far is that from you?"

"Oh, that's a good horse-ride."

"Is it? You go by horse do you?"

"Father does."

"Do you go?"

"No."

"You don't. You've never been to Exeter?"

"Father took me some time ago."

"He did?"

"When I was a little girl."

"And you have no other brothers or sisters."

"No, just Tom." (At no time during this or any subsequent recordings did Sally ever lapse in her Devon accent.)

"And what do you want to do when you get older, Sally?"

"Oh, I s'ppose I'll get married."

"You will? Have you any boy-friends now . . . any gentlemen friends . . . any boys do you know?"

"No, no one in partic'lar."

"But you have a few? You know a lot of people, do you?"

"Just the boys on the different farms."

"I see. Right Sally, I want you now to come forward a little in time and you're getting a little older. You're coming forward in time . . . coming forward in time . . . and you are now twenty-five ... you are now twenty-five and the year is 1741. You are now twenty-five and the year is 1741. In fact, today is your twenty-fifth birthday, Sally. Today you are twenty-five. [As this was a progression within a regressive I exaggerated the repetition technique to ensure a successful result.] How old are you, Sally?"

"I'm twenty-five." (Her voice immediately sounded more mature.)

"And what day is it? What is the date?"

"It's June." (Slightly hesitant.)

"June . . . what date?"

"June the fourth." (Peggy told me some time after that 4 June has no significance for her at all in her present lifetime.)

"I see, June 4th, 1741. Is it a nice day?"

"Fair . . . fair to middling."

"I see, and what is your full name?"

"It's Sally."

"Sally what?"

"Sally Barnes."

"Sally Barnes?"

"Yes."

"You're Mrs Sally Barnes, are you?"

"Oh yes, sir." (With great enthusiasm.)

"How long have you been married, Sally?"

"Six years."

"You've been married for six years, have you?"

"Yes sir."

"So you were about nineteen when you got married?"

"Yes sir." (I don't know why she called me 'sir.' It was most probably part of her character to be polite and respectful. Quite a different personality from Peggy was emerging, with mannerisms and expressions all typical of Sally.)

"And have you any children?"

"Yes, two."

"Tell me their names, please."

"Terry, the little boy."

"Yes."

"And Mary."

"Yes."

"She's the girl."

"And what's your husband's name, Sally?"

"Is Sam." (She said "Is" not "It's".)

"Sam, and what work does he do?"

"Oh, he's on a farm."

"And where do you live?"

"We live with my mother and my father."

"Where's that?"

"Why . . . near Exeter."

"I see."

"By the Exe."

"Have you ever been down to the sea?"

"Just once."

"How far is it to the sea? Is it a long way?"

"Well . . . [pronounced *Warl*] . . . fair to middling."

"And how do you go? When you went down to the sea, how did you go?"

"Oh, we went in the gig." (Her reply was quick and confident.)

"You went in the gig, did you? Was it nice?"

"Oh yes."

"Right. Sally . . . you're getting older and older . . . you're going forward a little in time . . . you're going forward a little in time. In fact, you're going forward now to your thirty-fifth

birthday. Today you are thirty-five. [She took a deep breath.]
Today is the fourth of June. Today is the fourth of June and
today you are thirty-five. How old are you, Sally?"

"I'm thirty-five." (A marked maturity in her voice.)

"And what is your full name?"

"Sally Barnes."

"And your husband's name is . . .?"

"I told you that." (She was quite sad.)

"Sam, is it?"

"Aye." (Almost as if she resented answering.)

"And you're still living on the farm, are you?"

"Aye. My mother and my father's dead now." (I now
understood the reason for her sadness.)

"How long have they been dead?"

"Oh, not a very long time. I still feel sad."

"Do you? And how about Tom, what's happened to Tom?"

"Oh, he went away to sea."

"He went away to sea? A long time ago?"

"Oh yes, a long time ago."

"And how about your children?"

"Oh, they're growing big now."

"How old are they, please?"

"Oh my! I just never remember, 'til I sit and work it out."

"Never mind. Right Sally, I want you to come forward in
time. You're getting older and older . . . coming forward in
time, and you are now forty-five years of age. Today is your
forty-fifth birthday . . . Today is your forty-fifth birthday. It is
the fourth of June and today you are forty-five. How old are
you Sally?"

"I'm forty-five." (Her voice was much older.)

"And you still live where you did years ago?"

"Oh aye, yes. I don't want to go nowhere else now."

"And how's Sam?"

"Oh, he's still well, still busy . . . gets a few twinges in his
back."

"How old is Sam? You're forty-five. How old is Sam?"

"Oh, Sam is fifty."

"I see, and how about Mary and the boy? How are the
children?"

"Oh, they're married now and gone away."

"Who did Mary get married to?"

"Oh, she had such a lot of boy-friends. Oh why! it were Dick."

"I see, and how about . . . I've forgotten the name of your boy. What was his name?" (I asked this question to see if she would be consistent, a ruse I used from time to time during my investigations.)

"Terry." (Without hesitation.)

"And who did he marry?"

"Oh, he married Janie."

"I see, and where . . . [but she interrupted me]."

"She'm a pretty girl, she'm." (Sally's character was getting more and more established and it seemed to me, even at this early stage, that the things she recalled more clearly and readily were events which had a strong emotional content.)

"I see. Right Sally, I want you to go forward in time and you're getting older and older. You're going forward in time . . . going forward in time . . . and now, today is your fifty-fifth birthday. Today you are fifty-five. Sally Barnes, today you are fifty-five and it is the fourth of June. Going forward to your fifty-fifth birthday, Sally Barnes. [She took a deep breath.] Today you are fifty-five and it is the fourth of June. [Another advantage of the repetition technique was the fact that it followed the lines of trance production and in this manner helped to promote an even deeper state of hypnosis as we progressed.] How old are you?"

"I'm fifty-five. The time's going on." (Her voice became progressively older as I advanced her age, actually older than someone of a similar age in the twentieth century. That is to be expected.)

"And are you well? Do you enjoy good health?"

"Oh yes . . . yes . . . I like to sit awhile now, sometimes."

"And how's Sam?"

"Oh, he's too you know. Fine one day, not so fine the next. You know how they get."

"And do you ever see much of Terry and Mary?"

"Oh, they come from time to time, you know."

"Where's Terry living, please?"

"Well he went away down to Cornwall, he did." (Pronounced *Carnwarl*.)

"And has he any children?"

"Yes, two."

"Boys or girls?"

"Well, they'm twins, one boy, one girl."

"And what are their names?"

"Christopher and . . . and . . . [she hesitated] . . . oh! . . . oh! John."

"You said one boy and one girl, did you? [She hesitated again.] Did you say he had twins, a boy and a girl?"

"Yes . . . he had." (She sounded puzzled.)

"Well, if one's Christopher and one's John, how about the girl?"

"Oh, that's Christopher John and Anne."

"I see. I see."

"My memory's getting awful bad these days, oh dear."

"And where does Mary live?"

"Oh, she lives handy in a farm, but she'm busy."

"Right, Sally Barnes. I want you to go forward in time. You are going forward in time, forward in time, forward in time and now this is your sixtieth birthday. You are sixty years old today. It is the fourth of June and today you are sixty. [Previously I had gone forward at ten-yearly intervals. As the expectancy of life was shorter in the eighteenth century than the present time, I took her forward only five years.] How old are you Sally?"

"I'm sixty today, sixty . . . tch, tch, tch." (The ageing of her voice was remarkable.)

"Many happy returns."

"Oh, thank'ee kindly."

"And how's Sam. Is he well?"

"No, he's not at all well, poor old Sam ain' . . . no."

"What's the trouble with him?"

"Oh, just old age, I think."

"Does he do much work now?"

"No, he has some men to help on the farm."

"And you're quite well?"

"Well, y'know, fine for a bit and not so fine." (She pronounced the word *Foin*.)

"I'm sorry about that. Sally, you're going forward in time another five years. You're going forward in time another five years and today you are sixty-five. Today you are sixty-five and it is the fourth of June. How old are you, Sally Barnes?"

"I'm sixty-five." (Very much older.)

"How old are you?"

"Sixty-five, I think."

"And are you well?"

"Oh, I don't remember things very much, you know."

"And how's Sam, how about Sam?"

"Oh, me poor Sam, oh, he's gone is me poor Sam!"

"I am sorry. How long has he been gone?"

"Oh, just two years."

"And what did he die from, Sally?"

"It was his heart in the end, you know." (Her voice was subdued and sad.)

"Are you living alone?"

"Well, there's the lads that help on the farm and me children come and me grandchildren. Oh, there seems such a lot of noise sometimes . . . such a lot of noise, but they mean to be kind."

"And Terry and Mary are well?"

"Oh yes, yes, they'm well."

"Right Sally, you're going forward in time just a little. You're going forward in time just a little, just a few years and you're getting a little older. You're going forward in time and you are now seventy. Sally Barnes, you are now seventy. This is the fourth of June and you are now seventy. Sally Barnes you are now seventy. How old are you Sally? [There was no reply. She lay very still. I waited a few moments and repeated the question.] How old are you Sally?. . . You are seventy. [Again no reply. I assumed that she was no longer alive at seventy.] Sally Barnes, I want you to go back in time a little to your sixty-seventh birthday. Sally Barnes, I want you to go back in time to your sixty-seventh birthday . . . sixty-seventh birthday . . . it is the fourth of June . . . it is the fourth of June, 1793. [Actually, this was an error. If she had been seventeen in 1733, then her year of birth was 1716 and the date of her sixty-seventh birthday would be 1783, but this did not seem to affect the regression as I had emphasized her age, sixty-seven, and not so much the year.] This is the fourth of June . . . the fourth of June. [She took a deep breath.] Today is the fourth of June and today you are sixty-seven. Today you are sixty-seven. How old are you, Sally?"

"I'm sixty-seven." (Her voice was very old and very tired.)

"And are you well?"

"No, I'm in me bed."

"What's the trouble, dear?"

"Well, I don' know. I jus' don' feel so well some'ow. I feel so tired . . . so tired."

"And the children?"

"All me good chil'en, they all come an' see Oi sometimes. Ah, they good chil'en."

"Sally, you're going forward in time just one year. You're going forward in time just one year and today is the fourth of June. It is your sixty-eight birthday. It is sixty-eight years after the day you were born. Sixty-eight years old. How old are you Sally? [No reply.] How old are you Sally? [Again no reply. Presumably she had died less than a year after her sixty-seventh birthday.] Sally, you're going back in time just a little. You're going back in time just a little. You're going back in time to your sixty-seventh birthday again. You're going back again to your sixty-seventh birthday. It's the fourth of June and today you are sixty-seven. How old are you, Sally Barnes?"

"Oh, I'm . . . oh, I'm sixty-seven." (Once again very old and tired.)

"And you're not feeling too good, eh?"

"No, I don' feel good at all. Me 'ead is bad, you know. My poor 'ead."

"Have you seen a doctor?"

"Oh apothecary comes, aye 'e comes."

"Who comes?"

"The apothecary comes."

"And what does he do for you, dear?"

"Oh, 'e gives me potions and such but it don't seem to do no good some'ow. No, it don't seem to do no good."

"What is the name of the apothecary?"

"Oh, I think you'll have to ask someone. I . . . er . . . I can't really remember . . . mm . . . mm . . ."

"Never mind."

"No, I cannot, my poor 'ead."

"What does he say is wrong with you?"

"I ain' know, 'e goes outside and 'e whispers and I can't 'ear what 'e says. But it's me poor 'ead, aye, yes. I'll be glad to go and see my Sam." (Her West Country accent was now at its strongest.)

"Would you?"

"Oh, my Sam's waiting for me there."

"How do you know?"

"Oh, I seen 'im!" (She sounded a little more cheerful as she said this with a suggestion of hopeful expectancy.)

"You have? Tell me, Sally."

"Oh, 'e stands there, a-noddin' and a-smilin' and a-beckonin' at me, [and then very tenderly] oh, 'e does, me dear old Sam."

"How long have you been seeing him, Sally?"

"Oh, just for a little while now. A few weeks, I guess. 'e knows my 'ead's bad, 'e knows."

"Do you think you'll soon be joining him?"

"Oh, I must. 'e's waiting for me. I can't wait too long now."

"How long do you think you'll have to wait, dear?"

"Oh, not very long. Me head's been bad now for a while and I feel so tired . . . so tired."

"Right, Sally. I want you to go forward in time just three months. Go forward in time just three months ... three months forward in time . . . three months forward in time and it is the fourth of September . . . it is now the fourth of September and you were sixty-seven, [In my excitement at what was happening I forgot whether I had said sixty-seven or sixty-eight and so I had a quick, whispered consultation with Bill. 'Was it sixty-seven?' Bill said 'Sixty-seven.' I continued to Sally:] you were sixty-seven three months ago. You were sixty-seven three months ago. How old are you, Sally? [She made no sign of answering.] How old are you dear? [Still no answer.] Sally, I want you to go back a little in time now . . . a few weeks . . . just a few weeks, to the day that you joined Sam. Go back now, Sally, a few weeks to the day that you joined Sam. This is the day that you joined Sam. You were sixty-seven on the fourth of June. Now, what is the date now, Sally? This is the day that you are joining Sam. Tell me, dear."

"My Sam." (Very weak and almost incoherent.)

"Do you know?"

"No." (Very faint.)

"Is it long after your birthday?"

"No, 'cos the flowers is still livin' in the vase . . . no." (Her voice was now almost a whisper. I had to hold the microphone barely an inch from her lips.)

"How do you feel, dear?"

"Oh, I feel kind-a peaceful today . . . kind-a peaceful."

"Do you think something wonderful is going to happen today?"

"Oh yes, I think . . . I think my Sam's a-comin' for me."

"Can you see him?"

"Aye, I can. His face is all smilin' and bright . . . aye, I can."

"And how do you feel? How's your head?"

"Oh, that don' hurt no more."

"It doesn't?"

"No." (Very faintly.)

"Sally, you will be able to hear me and although you are going to join Sam, although you are joining Sam, although you are leaving this earth and joining Sam, you will be able to hear me and you will still be able to answer me . . . and you will be able to tell me about the wonderful reunion you have with Sam. Can you see him now, clearer? Tell me more about it."

"Mm . . . mm." (She could hardly move her lips and was obviously very weak.)

"Tell me, Sally. [She tried to mouth words for a few moments but failed.] Go back to an hour before you joined Sam . . . one hour before you joined Sam and tell me . . . tell me, Sally, how do you feel and what do you see . . . one hour before you join Sam."

"All my children . . ." (A mere whisper.)

"All your children . . ."

"All my children . . ."

"Tell me more. [Her breathing was laboured.] And you're going to join Sam now, are you?"

"Yeh . . . yeh . . ."

"There's Sam, isn't he?"

"Yeh . . ." (The faintest of whispers.)

"He's smiling, isn't he?"

"Yeh . . . [scarcely audible] 'im takin' my 'and."

"Yes . . .? (and then her last dying gasp . . .!)

The three of us in the room stared at the silent figure on the couch. I bent over her. She was very still and breathing gently. I could feel my pulse racing. I had hoped for but not expected what had just happened. I was absolutely and completely unprepared for the effect it had on me. Sally had just died. Peggy Bailey was there on the couch in deep trance. Yet Peggy seemed remote. It was Sally, her life, her times, her death, which seemed so real, so present. Bill was white-faced. Joan had tears in her eyes. Had I, perhaps, lost all contact with Sally? I was soon to find out. I continued:

"Right, Sally, I want you to go back now to your thirtieth birthday. Today, Sally Barnes you are thirty. How old are you, Sally?"

"I'm thirty today." (A quick, bright and cheerful answer. The healthy voice of Sally in her prime.)

"And how do you feel?"

"Oh, I feel wonderful! It's grand to be thirty."

"And is it a nice day?"

"Well, him kind of misty."

"What are you going to do today?"

"Oh, I don't know. I reckon the children 'll make my tea for me and give me a nice little rest."

"How's Sam?"

"Oh, him fine . . . oh my goodness, him fine!"

"Thank you, Sally. Thank you very much indeed, and I look forward to meeting you again soon."

"Yes sir."

I felt a surge of relief as I switched off the tape-recorder. I sat there staring ahead of me for a full two minutes without saying a word. What an incredible experience! To the people who said it had all been done before the response must be "so has a solo flight but there is nothing like the awesome first time of doing it yourself."

Having composed myself, I brought Peggy back to the present time, reidentified her as Peggy Bailey, and woke her up out of her trance.

"Did I go under all right?" asked Peggy.

"Quite satisfactorily," I understated.

"I think your car nerves will be quite cured by now."

"Does that mean I don't have to come back for more hypnosis?" she asked.

I threw a hasty glance at Bill. I had to see her again for further investigations. We couldn't stop now. Bill read my thoughts and gave a quick nod. "Only if you want to," I said hopefully.

"Oh yes," she said. "I always feel so lovely and relaxed afterwards, even if I can't remember a single thing that happened. Are you quite sure I went under?"

"Quite, quite sure." I said.

As soon as the Baileys left, Joan and I played and replayed the tape. Now I was an objective listener, hearing about Sally's life in the eighteenth century. Her deathbed experiences were very moving, to say the least. Of course, it was obvious to me that I could have made far more searching enquiries of her by probing for more factual information. But I was well satisfied with my first 'solo flight into the past'. Having opened the door I could always go through it again and discover more about Sally Fraser. It seemed quite incredible that by using such a straightforward hypnotic technique I had actually made her abreact all these memories of a 'previous life'. I wondered if she had other 'lives' that could be discovered in the same way? What should I do at the next session? Make further investigation of Sally Fraser, or try other time periods in the hope of meeting other 'personalities'? I decided to do the latter. I think this was an obvious choice. I wondered how many different 'lives' I could unfold. If I were successful in this I could then revisit each personality at a later date. I was well aware that this apparent production of a previous life may not necessarily be due to Peggy Bailey's remembering herself as Sally Fraser. There were other explanations, the chief contender being known as 'role taking'. This is where the hypnotized person deceives him or herself (and frequently the inexperienced hypnotist) by assuming the personality of a character in a different century, using information from the storehouse of the subconscious to produce facts and events

with which to embellish the 'story'. If this were the reason for
Sally Fraser I wondered if Peggy Bailey would be able to
reproduce the story she had given me. Very likely so, as the
subconscious memory is profoundly accurate. All these
thoughts went through my mind as after listening to the tape a
number of times that evening I eventually put it carefully
away. Whatever the explanation for Sally Fraser I decided
even at that early stage to try not to commit myself at any time
to a personal verdict, but to pursue the investigations to the
best of my ability and in due course to invite a third party to
evaluate my material. For I was determined to investigate this
fascinating field. At a later date, after I had compiled a library
of Peggy Bailey tape-recordings, I did, in fact, invite carefully
selected groups of people to listen to the recordings and to give
their unbiased opinions. These included a doctor, a
psychiatrist, a hypnotist, a solicitor, an obstetrician, a
television and film director, the famous stage, screen and
television actress Diana Rigg, and a renowned psychic
researcher, Peter Underwood. This then would be an
appropriate point in the book for Peter Underwood to start his
comments and observations.

But what of Peggy Bailey's reactions? As far as she was
concerned she had received hypnosis for her car phobia and
had no knowledge whatsoever of having been regressed to
childhood or to Sally Fraser, or even that a recording had been
made. She realized that she was now completed cured and so I
had to offer her some rational reason for continuing to come
for hypnosis so regularly. I was completely honest with her
without disclosing too much. I told her that as she was such a
good subject, a fact she already knew, I would like to carry out
a few harmless experiments over a period of time. I said that
the nature of the experiments was such that I preferred her not
to know what they were until I had carried them out. To this
she readily agreed. "I owe it to you, Leonard," she said, "for
helping me, and as I do feel so relaxed afterwards I always
look forward to the next session." I certainly looked forward to
it no less than she.

4
Assessment and Discussion I

Before continuing with Leonard Wilder's account of his experimentation with Peggy Bailey, it may be of value to consider some of the topics and implications and some of the questions that come to mind on the material that has been obtained so far.

From a psychical researcher's point of view there are many aspects to be considered. When investigating any paranormal phenomenon it is often a good plan not to question the paranormal original of the activity in the first instance and to concentrate instead on taking copious notes followed by control and verification.

In the case of Peggy Bailey, Leonard Wilder has explained in detail the circumstances that led up to his attempt to regress this subject who had already shown herself to be fully co-operative – perhaps even suggestible – and an eminently suitable subject for experimentation and possible regression.

It was not until March 1974 that I actually met Peggy and Bill Bailey and on that occasion Leonard Wilder, for my express benefit, began from the beginning and went through the whole careful and elaborate technique of hypnotizing Peggy Bailey. Let me say at once that there is no doubt whatever that Leonard Wilder can hypnotize Peggy Bailey. I have ample proof of this and during the session in which I took part, in the presence of my wife, Leonard Wilder's wife Joan, and Peggy Bailey's husband Bill, Leonard Wilder carried out several experiments which precluded any possibility of conscious fraud on the part of Peggy Bailey. As a researcher I am satisfied that Peggy Bailey was hypnotized and she responded completely to Leonard Wilder's will in my presence. That being so I see no reason to think that there is any doubt whatever that he was equally successful in hypnotizing Peggy Bailey some seventeen years previousiy.

Whether Peggy Bailey's alleged and apparent previous lines have any basis in fact is a different matter entirely and one that can only be determined, if at all, after considerable research, patience and consideration of the evidence produced. At this stage however it may be pertinent to consider a number of points that arise from the material obtained so far.

Early in the first regression when Peggy Bailey talked of her childhood, first as a thirteen-year-old schoolgirl, then at the age of six, and finally about three years old, the change in intonation and evident intelligence is strikingly apparent on the tape-recording fortunately made at the time. Leonard Wilder has remarked on the very interesting phenomenon of the subject taking a very deep breath, something that nearly always accompanied a change in age or different personality.

When a hypnotist *suggests* to an unhypnotized subject that he or she will take on the role of another person when they are hypnotized, this deep breathing *never* occurs. Furthermore 'conscious' role-taking is completely unconvincing, the hypnotized person obviously searching hesitantly for incidents to tell to the hypnotist to convince him of the adopted character; there is no spontaneity and nothing resembling the continuity, ease of delivery and apparently open co-operation that is so convincing in the Peggy Bailey regressions. Whether of course Peggy Bailey is *unconsciously* role-taking is another matter.

It is, I think, significant that in the final stages of that first regression, when Peggy Bailey is talking as a child of three and Leonard Wilder tries to develop the converstaion, the 'child' suddenly and without explanation withdraws her co-operation. This is exactly the action of a child with a stranger. For a little while he or she will talk, then suddenly and for no apparent reason the *rapport* will be lost and the child will abruptly turn away. This *is* the typical reaction of a child; it is completely in character. And it is not unfair to ask whether, if this was true regression, would Peggy Bailey revert to role-taking later?

There is certainly evidence to suggest that this initial

regression was a true one and it is significant that the deep
breathing at the beginning of each regression is already
established. Notice too the pronunciation of the words
"Thwee" (for three), "Peg-gy", slowly and with a suggestion
of shyness and the slight hesitation over the surname: all this
is typical of a child. Was it spontaneous acting – or what?

Leonard Wilder's whole approach to what must have been
an astonishing experience is remarkably sensible and level-
headed. I have been careful in my evaluation of the Peggy
Bailey regressions to discount my knowledge of Leonard
Wilder over a period of some twenty years, although I did not
get to really know him and his family until after his lecture on
these regressions at The Ghost Club in London and at a
conference at Oxford in 1972. Before then I had considerable
admiration for his ability and achievements as a dental
surgeon and I have always been conscious of his fair-
mindedness, open but critical approach, and knowledge of
several facets of psychic phenomena.

His interest in the experiences of people who have been very
near to death is evidenced by the incidents he recounts and I
may say in passing that I too knew Howard Livens and heard
his experience first-hand. I have also met Philip Saville who
told me of his near-fatal accident. Jeremy Lloyd's out-of-the-
body experience was not of course associated with near death
and there are many, many examples of such experiences in the
records of psychic research that defy a rational explanation;
but to return to Peggy Bailey.

In the first regression to 'Sally Fraser' it is important to bear
in mind that the hypnotist was *not* familiar at all with the
Exeter district. In fact he had only travelled along the A30. It
would seem that wherever Peggy Bailey or 'Sally Fraser'
obtained the information, and the Devon accent, she did not
obtain it from the hypnotist. It must be admitted that the
information obtained in indefinite and very localized, but then
a young girl of seventeen in 1733, living on a remote farm in
Devon, *would* have a very limited and localized knowledge and
in all probability would know very little about the country
outside her immediate surroundings. It is evident that she is
striving to be definite on occasions and this raises for the first
time in the mind of an objective researcher the question: Is the

psychic entity itself a fantasy, or is it a separate personality? At this stage it is a question that must remain unanswered.

One wonders why she chose to return at the age of seventeen. Perhaps because this is an attractive age for a girl, an age that many girls look back on as a time of innocence and uncomplicated happiness. It is arguable that many women, if they could choose to return for a while, might pick on the period when they were about seventeen. Whatever the reason, the first 'appearance' of 'Sally Fraser' was at seventeen years of age; a bright and happy girl looking forward to life and whatever it might hold for her. How different from the 'Sally Fraser' later on.

There is also the authentic Devon accent which *never* lapses while the character is present; the phraseology and intonation, strikingly convincing on tape and faithfully reproduced by Leonard Wilder in the script. West Country people who have heard the tape-recording have insisted that the voice is completely authentic.

That first recording is a remarkable achievement when one considers the fact that Leonard Wilder had no idea whether the experiment would prove successful and he had no questions or ideas prepared. Even so he made very few mistakes. Perhaps he ought not to have suggested that the communicator was *Mrs* Sally Barnes when she was twenty-three since this was feeding her with information; and it might have been interesting if he had asked who he (the hypnotist) was, but this might have been confusing and caused unnecessary complications. In any case these are minor points and by and large it is difficult to conceive anyone, in the given circumstances, doing better than Leonard Wilder – and obtaining and preserving a recording of the whole affair.

The quality and varying intonation of the voice is often strikingly significant, as for example when a sadness in the delivery of the words is noticeable *before* the reasons are given for the subject being sad: sometimes this only becomes apparent several questions later. This raises such complicated questions as whether the subject knows what the hypnotist is going to ask her before he does so, or even knows himself! Perhaps this aspect of the regression points to role-taking, but what powers are at work that can produce answers to questions in a manner that only makes sense when the subject is regressed to a different period five years later?

So many questions to ask. So many suggestions that genuine regression to a previous life seems to be more easy to accept than elaborate theories involving conscious or unconscious role-taking, multiple personality, even temporary possession. So much that is completely in character and much of it unlikely to be known to Peggy Bailey in her normal state. Words like 'gig' and 'apothecary' set the scene perfectly; yet they are produced immediately without any hesitation and no prompting or guiding. The complete spontaneity of the whole thing is tremendously convincing, yet can it really be genuine regression? Hardened by continual examples of conscious and unconscious fraud in various branches of psychic research, the researcher remains sceptical and searches for yet more proof and indisputable evidence of the existence of the alleged communicators.

At certain times, and particularly during that first regression to 'Sally Fraser', the hypnotist is endeavouring to contact 'something' – whatever it may be – that lives on after the death of the physical body and when (after several attempts) he is unsuccessful, he tries to get a death-bed scene. This he does by going backwards and forewards in time until he reaches the required period; whatever the explanation it is a remarkable achievement, and encouraged by this apparent success he attempts further regressions to other lives, but I will deal with that later on. While survival after death may not have been proved to the satisfaction of everyone, the search for that proof suggests very strongly that at least something survives the disintegration of the body; something that might be called a soul, but what is the genesis of the soul? We tend to consider that a newborn child has a new soul, but does it? It may be that the soul and the body grow together for a time until the body is worn out, when the soul seeks and finds a new body. Whatever the answer, we have to accept that we do not know the genesis of the soul. One wonders whether communication of some kind might be possible with a foetus at different stages of development. In a way this is already to be found in Tibet where belief in reincarnation predominates, and in the periodical search for the reincarnated Dalai Lama, the favoured child is tested by attempting to choose articles from a collection, some of which have belonged to the former Dalai Lama. There are many byways to be explored in the search for evidence for reincarnation.

Many people would adjudge a further pointer to true regression in the 'Sally Fraser' experiment to be the expression: "Oh why! it were Dick." This typical expression comes through after apparent thought on the subject, which is either role-taking or acting of a very high order or it strongly suggests true regression. It is interesting to speculate that the hesitation in naming Dick might originate from an unconscious alienation between 'her' and Dick, as there often is between a mother and the young man who 'takes' her daughter away. In this particular case it is surely significant that there is no similar 'hold-back' when 'she' is asked about her own son, Terry, only seconds later; or in respect of her daughter Mary. It may be quite wrong to suggest that 'Sally Fraser' and her son-in-law did not always see eye-to-eye, but if this was so, then it is a common enough occurrence and the momentary amnesia of his name is a well-known psychological evasion.

It is noticeable that the voice of 'Sally Fraser' at the apparent age of fifty-five sounded much older than the voice of a woman of that age does today. (In 1771 fifty-five was a good age for a woman; since then the life expectancy has progressively increased.) But would this 'older voice' idea have occurred to Peggy Bailey? It might be thought to be unlikely.

Another authentic touch is when the hypnotist tries to trip up the subject on the question of her grandchildren which she has said were twins, a boy and a girl; yet she has given the names as Christopher and (after some hesitation) John. She is not to be confused however and quietly repeats the two boys' names as that of the grandson. It is a common practice for grandmothers to use their grandchildren's two christian names, but would a role-taking and conscious woman think of this way of extraditing herself from the predicament in which she had become involved? She seems to have responded with remarkable authenticity to a situation that she had never actually experienced.

A little later there is another interesting point that may not be immediately apparent to everyone. As a prematurely-aged woman of sixty-five 'Sally Barnes' speaks kindly but knowledgeably of her grandchildren: "there seems such a lot of noise sometimes . . . such a lot of noise, but they mean to be kind." Peggy Bailey was at this time a healthy married woman of thirty-five without children, and if this was role-taking it might perhaps represent a suppressed longing for a child. Yet the impression obtained from the tape-recording by the words that are spoken is that of an elderly lady being a little annoyed by children's noise. Not, one might think, an aspect that would come readily in role-taking in the given circumstances.

In any summing-up of the initial 'Sally Fraser' regression it seems fair to say that if this was role-taking, it was extremely effective and impressive for Peggy Bailey has never acted in her normal life, and furthermore *everything* the subject said and the way she said it had a quite remarkable authenticity. At this stage no psychical researcher would say more.

I recall that Leonard Wilder recounted to me the shock he had when he received no reply at the stage when he suggested that 'Sally Fraser' was seventy years of age. This was the very first time that this had happened; it was, as he put it, "an eerie experience". It is, I feel, significant that he quickly recovered, and realizing that 'Sally Fraser' had not apparently reached 'three score years and ten', he suggested that she was sixty-seven and was reassured by the familiar Devon accent, although noticeably older and seemingly tired.

In retrospect it might have been wiser had his question, a little later, been phrased something like, "How do you feel?" rather than the suggestive and loaded "And you're not feeling too good?" which brought the immediate reply, "No, I don' feel good at all . . ." But on the other hand 'she' had already said she had not been too well at sixty-seven years of age so it is fair to say that she would perhaps be unlikely to feel better later.

Shortly afterwards came one of the big and possibly significant surprises of the whole regression. In reply to the sympathetic enquiry "Have you seen a doctor?" came "Oh the apothecary comes . . ."

The year is 1783. Only nine years earlier the Society of Apothecaries passed a resolution limiting its members to those who were practising apothecaries, i.e. medical practitioners.

Originally an apothecary was a person who prepared and traded in drugs and in medieval England the apothecary flourished in the rising trade in drugs and spices from the East. Early in the seventeenth century a Society of Apothecaries was formed and they had the monopoly of buying and selling drugs within the city of London. So the apothecary became the pharmacist of the time, but soon they were not content to dispense the prescriptions of the physicians and bowing to public demand they began to treat the sick. Indeed, during the Great Plague of London in 1665 most of the physicians left the city while the apothecaries stayed and attended to the sick and dying. In 1783 there is no doubt that the apothecary would be the term used by most people for the medical practitioner who visited the sick and prescribed treatment, and it is fascinating to come across such a term unhesitatingly coming from the hypnotized Peggy Bailey – so completely in character with the personality of 'Sally Fraser' and so foreign to the present-day Peggy Bailey.

Again, in retrospect, when 'Sally Fraser' mentions that the apothecary "goes outside and 'e whispers and I can't 'ear what 'e says", it might have been interesting to ask *who* he whispered to; but on his first tremendously exciting experience of apparent regression, the hypnotist can be forgiven for not thinking of everything. All in all it is indisputable that he made a really good first attempt at regression, overall an excellent job of work, and one wonders how many hypnotists in the same circumstances would have done as well. The apparent authenticity, down to the smallest detail, is quite remarkable. The flowers still in the vase, for instance; how very significant. Would anyone consciously role-taking really think of saying such a thing in an attempt to establish the role?

It is possible to again criticize the hypnotist when he asks whether "something wonderful is going to happen" that day. Undoubtedly this can be construed as 'feeding' the subject – but then again, he had to retain *rapport* with her and in view of all that had gone before, it is perhaps understandable that he presumed that there would be a reunion.

I also think it is only fair to draw attention to the interesting and very proper anxiety on the part of the hypnotist to obtain Peggy Bailey's permission to continue the experiment at a later date. It is important from every point of view to establish that there is nothing whatever unethical about this strange, absorbing and increasingly remarkable venture into the unknown.

In apparent regression 'role-taking', conscious or unconscious, must be considered. It is known that some subjects, to please the hypnotist, unconsciously *assume* a character and completely mislead the unsuspecting investigator. This has without doubt happened in the past. And in the present case . . .? I asked Leonard Wilder what would happen if he told Peggy Bailey, while she was hypnotized, that unless 'Sally Fraser' was authentic and real, then she would be completely inhibited from fabricating any alleged story of any part of 'her' life. He told me that he had in fact done just this – and 'Sally Fraser' was still produced!

With other hypnotic subjects Leonard Wilder devised the procedure of 'deliberate fantasy' where the subject was instructed to pretend to be someone else in a different century. Having been given time to construct a story they were told to act out the role to the best of their ability. The results have *never* been convincing. The preliminary deep breathing before each apparent change in time was always absent; there was no ageing of the voice; there was always hesitation in answering and there was nothing approaching the spontaneity of the 'Sally Fraser' regressions.

On the other hand many people have a remarkable ability to store information subconsciously. Some can casually glance at a page in a book and their minds store information that they have no conscious knowledge of possessing. Only under hypnosis can this information be brought out. In 'role-taking' such material could be the origin of information that seems to come from a regression in age.

There is no doubt that 'Sally Fraser's' voice, the accent, ageing and use of vocabulary, are all very authentic. If this is *conscious* role-taking, it is a notable and impressive performance. I recall hearing the tape-recording on one occasion in the presence of actress Diana Rigg who commented that if this *was* reincarnation, it was a truly remarkable recording. She discounted role-taking as being even more remarkable, for (in her opinion) to produce such a brilliant piece of acting could only be done by an experienced actress whereas in Peggy Bailey we have an ordinary housewife with, as we have established, no experience whatever of dramatic art.

Nevertheless the inventive capacity of the human mind is continually amazing to investigators of psychic phenomena. In 1972 a group of members of the Toronto Society for Psychical Research decided to attempt to construct a ghost, following considerable discussion on the nature of ghosts and speculation as to whether most ghosts were in fact conjured up from the minds of the beholders. Accordingly an entirely imaginary character was decided upon: an aristocratic Englishman, living in the middle of the seventeenth century, married and having an affair with a beautiful gypsy girl, and so on. It was decided that the imaginary character, named Philip, made no effort to defend the girl when she was accused of witchcraft and burned alive; that he had been reincarnated several times, and that once every hundred years or so his ghost was seen at his home, pacing the battlements in remorse and despair. It was theorized that if he could materialize and be reassured that the gypsy girl had forgiven him, he would be at rest.

The group, five female and three male, spent a lot of time inventing and elaborating the story and then started holding sittings in a circle around a table and meditating. In the summer of 1973 (following study of work on similar lines carried out by K.J. Batcheldor in 1966, C. Brookes-Smith and D.W. Hunt in 1970, and C. Brookes-Smith in 1973) it was decided to try a different approach and an atmosphere of jollity and relaxation was introduced. Soon table raps were heard when certain songs were sung and these raps became progressively louder and more obvious after the group addressed the table as 'Philip' and after the procedure of one rap for 'Yes' and two for 'No' was adopted.

Questions were asked regarding Philip, his likes and dislikes, his habits and customs, and the table responded;

nearly always in accordance with the invented personality of
Philip. Later, some four weeks after the raps had first been
produced, the table began to move around the room in
random fashion. It would, on occasions, shoot across the room
at great speed and when the experimenters, catching up with
it and standing round the table, would continue their
questions, raps would come from it with force and
intelligence. Once a member of the Society not associated with
the experiment came into the room and witnessed a loud rap,
and once the vice-president of the Society also witnessed the
rapping, which was also heard by many sceptical people not
associated with the project; as was the movement of the table.
Everyone was satisfied that the raps and the movements were
produced paranormally. The experiments continue and I am
indebted to Dr A.R.G. Owen, vice-president of the Toronto
Society for Psychical Research and life member of The Ghost
Club, for bringing these fascinating experiments to my notice
and for permission to publish this résumé from a report
published in *New Horizons*, Volume 1, Number 3, dated
January 1974.

And now back to Leonard Wilder, Peggy Bailey, and more
attempts at regression to a bygone age . . .

5
Liza

I was to be a little frustrated in an attempt to arrange the next session with Peggy. For several weeks it was never quite convenient to find a suitable time for the four of us to meet. Bill was either away flying off somewhere or I was working late or engaged on a post-graduate course. We did, however, arrange a meeting rather late one evening. I had had a tiring day and by the time I had hypnotized Peggy I had overlooked my plan to attempt a regression to a possible other 'life'. I soon had her in deep trance. I regressed her to childhood and asked her to go back in time to when she was someone else on this earth. Out of the corner of my eye I noticed Joan gesticulating. I turned my head. "You've forgotten to switch on the tape-recorder," she whispered. I hurriedly did so. I quickly returned to Peggy and asked her:

"What is your name?"

"I'm Liza!" (A raucous, cockney voice. What good luck. I'd found another personality, without even trying!)

"How old are you, Liza?

"I don't know." (Sullen and resentful.)

"Are you a very little girl?"

"No. I work in the kitchen." (She pronounced it *kitchin*.)

"How old are you?"

"I don't know." (Still resentful.)

"You don't know?"

"No."

"Got any names other than Liza?"

"No, they don't call me nothink else."

"Whose kitchen do you work in?"

"Cook's." (Her sullenness persisted.)

"And where is that?"

"I don't like cook!" (She ignored my question.)

"Don't you like cook?"

"No, I don't like cook!" (She accentuated the 'k' of 'cook' when she said the word, which seemed to amuse her.)

"What's her name?"

"I jes' call 'er cook..k."

"And where are you? What country is this?"

"Oh well, in the Smoke o' course."

"What town?"

"In London!" (Very raucous.)

"What part of London?"

"Oh, all in the posh!"

"Oh, I see, what district?"

"Piccadilly!" (A cockney drawl.)

"I see . . . well, thank you very much indeed."

At this point my telephone rang. I had wrapped a towel around the instrument to muffle the sound in the event of its ringing. I had removed an impacted wisdom tooth for a patient earlier that day and I anticipated that he may be calling me. I switched off the tape-recorder. It was, indeed, my patient and it was necessary for me to see him again, albeit quite late in the evening. Our long-awaited and very brief but exciting session had to be terminated at once. I brought Peggy back to the present and woke her up. Full of apologies, I arranged another meeting for the following Sunday afternoon, when we should all have much more time. As soon as they left I prepared to receive my dental patient.

Sunday afternoon arrived all too slowly. Soon Peggy was lying comfortably on the couch again. After an induction into deep trance followed by a brief regression to Peggy's early childhood, I was ready for another giant leap into the past. I decided to let Peggy's subconscious make the choice as to whether she produced Sally or Liza. I hoped, of course, that after the previous quick meeting it would be Liza again. I switched on the tape-recorder:

"I want you to go back much further in time, back, back, back, back in time before you were born Peggy Beeching. Going back, going back, you're going back in time, back, back, back when you were someone else on this earth. [She took a deep breath.] Right now, back, back, back. [She took another deep breath.] What's your name?"

"I'm Liza." (The same raucous voice as in the previous

short recording. She had chosen Liza again. I was delighted.)

"And how old are you, Liza?"

"I don't know."

"Where do you work?"

"In cook's kitchen."

"What's cook's name?"

"Mrs Bates, but I call 'er cook." (This was encouraging. In the previous session she had not remembered cook's name. I found that each time a subject was interrogated more information was forthcoming than during previous sessions. It was as though the past memory was being revived more and more each time.)

"And where do you work, what town?"

"Oh, I'm in the Smoke."

"What town's that?"

"Why, London o' course."

"And what part of London?"

"In a big 'ouse."

"Who owns the house?"

"A Lord." (Almost confidentially.)

"Lord what?"

"Lord Frobisher." (Quite proudly.)

"Oh, I see. What does he do?"

"Oh, Gawd knows . . . pots o' money."

"Has he got a wife?"

"Yers."

"And how long have you been working there?"

"Not very long. They got me from the Foundlings, you see."

'I see. Where was the Foundlings? Where was it, what part of London?'

"Millbank."

"Millbank?"

"Yus."

"Where do you work now, what part of London is that?"

"I'm in Piccadilly now."

"What's it like? Can you tell me what it looks like?"

"Ooh, big 'ouses y'know . . . one big 'ouse, bit of green, another big 'ouse, bit more green . . . you know." (She drawled the last two words. Her cockney character was becoming more and more established.)

"Ever been out of London?"

"Cor no! 'course I ain't."

"How about school? Do you ever go to school?"

"Ah, they used to teach us a few things."

"What was the name of the Foundlings?"

"I don't know ... [She sounded rather surprised that she did not know.] ... they just said they brung me from the Foundlings."

"How long ago was that? How old are you now?"

"I don't know. They seemed to think I might be about thirteen or something."

"Have you been there a long time with Mrs Bates?"

"No ... no, not very long, but blimey it don't 'arf seem a long time. Clips me round the ear she does, somethink shocking!" (I was beginning to like little Liza.)

"Who else is in the kitchen with you?"

"Oh, there's Mr blooming Jenkins, the butler. There's poor old Sid, the little lad, what cleans the boots. Oh, what a life, I dunno!"

"What's your second name? Have you got another name?"

"Well, I s'pose I must have, but I'm only ever called Liza. Suits them."

"You don't know what it is?"

"No. Don't know whether the Foundling knows. S'pose they would. I dunno."

"What do you do when you're not working?"

"Cor crikey, I'm always working!"

"What time do you get up?"

"'bout six, as a rule."

"And what do you do all day?"

"Oh, just anythink and everythink. Do the vegetables ... wash the pots up ... scrub the floors ... carry the water up and down. [In a sort of sing-song cockney.] Somebody always wantin' a barf. Imagine people always wantin' a barf, eh! Water, Liza! Water, Liza! Coo, my aching back!"

"What, at thirteen?"

"Yers. Would your back 'ad ached carrying all that water and down the stairs! Up one lot of stairs ... along the passage ... up another lot of stairs ... along the passage . . . then we get to where they 'ave their barf." (A likeable thirteen-year-old, facing up to an overwhelming world.)

"Liza, I want you to go forwad in time. You're getting a little older and you are going forward in time to your twentieth birthday. [She took a deep breath.] Liza, you have gone forward in time to your twentieth birday. Today Liza, you are twenty. How old are you, Liza?" (Still using the repetition technique and the check question.)

"Oh, I'm twenty now . . . least I think I'm twenty now. I'm not ever so sure how old I am, you see." (Even in these few words I noticed a marked improvement in her diction, as though she were making an effort to talk 'posh', as she might put it.)

"Where do you live?"

"I'm still in service, but I've gone up a lot now. [Carefully and with deliberation.] I'm me Lady's personal maid." (Proudly.)

"Still at the same place?"

"Oh yes. They've been very good to me, really. I've got my own little room now."

"How about Mrs Bates? What's happened to her?"

"Oh, she left. I think they've had one or two cooks since. I don't see them very much, you see. [The casual manner in which she told me this was amusing when compared with her earlier concern regarding her relationship with cook.] I'm Lady's personal maid now." (Very proudly.)

"I see. And how about Lord . . . er . . . what was his name?" (I attempted to catch her out.)

"Lord Frobisher." (Without hesitation.)

"How's he?"

"Oh, he's still busy, you know."

"Well? Keeping well?"

"Oh yes."

"How long have you been personal maid?"

"Couple of years now."

"That's good, is it?"

"What do you think of my education, what she's giving me?" (Trying to impress me.)

"Well, I must say you're speaking better."

"Oh, I'm pleased. I do try, really I do try." (I felt that she had said this more than once to Lady Frobisher during her 'education'.)

"Do you earn much money?"

"Ooh yes. I get ten shillings a week now."

"That's wonderful."

"Ooh yes, it is!"

"What were you getting at first, when you first started in the kitchen?"

"Oh, clips round the ear mostly!" (This lightning cockney wit always produced a roar of laughter from listeners to the recording. I had difficulty in controlling myself at the time.)

"And she's teaching you 'education', is she?"

"Well, she says I don't speak so very good, so she thought she'd better do something about it. So, when I brushes 'er 'air at night [a lapse!] she tells me 'ow I ought to speak, you see."

"Well, I'm glad you're getting on so well. Tell me, now that you've had a bit of education, what year is this?"

"Ooh, what year?"

"Mm . . . mm."

"Let me think . . . ooh . . . ooh dear, it's eight-er . . . ooh, ooh dear, ooh, do you mind, I can't think." (How very different was this Liza from Sally or Peggy.)

"You gave me something then, didn't you?"

"Yers." (In her agitation she was lapsing again.)

"Well, have a go . . . roughly." (I was trying to establish a date.)

"Roughly?" (She seemed encouraged.)

"Ten years either way, we don't really mind."

"Ah, wait a minute. 'er Ladyship was saying . . . ah, she was saying it was 1823. Yes, that's right, 1823."

"So, you were born about 1803, then were you? If you are about twenty?"

"Dear me, I don't know when I was born. Oh, it is terrible." (Without any feeling.)

"Well, if it's 1823 and you're about twenty, then you were born in 1803, weren't you? But it doesn't matter, does it?"

"Oh, was I? Oh tah! Oh, it's nice to know." (She was humouring me with this remark, as though she really could not understand why I was attaching so much significance to her year of birth.)

"Do you know when your birthday is?"

"No, I don't never 'ave a birthday."

"Right, Liza. I want you to go forward in time. Going forward in time ten years. Liza, you're going forward in time ten years. Going forward in time ten years [she took a deep breath] and now you are thirty. Liza, you are now thirty. Liza, you are thirty. How old are you, Liza?"

"I'm thir'y now." (Her voice was more mature and she had lost her 'education'.)

"Are you well?"

"Oh yes, I always 'ad good health."

"Where are you? Where do you live? What do you do?"

"I live in Lambeth y'know."

"Oh, have you left Lady Frobisher?"

"Well, 'course. I married 'arry Bloggs."

"How long ago?"

"Only three [pronounced *free*] years ago."

"Tell me about Harry?"

"Oh, he was a soldier."

"Tell me about him."

"I met him when I was out one day."

"Yes?"

"He looked ever so nice in his uniform, wiv 'is little round 'at, and 'is blue trousers and 'is nice red jacket."

"What rank?"

"Well, 'e was at Wellington Barracks."

"Is he still in the army?"

"Oh no, no, 'e goes to the market to work y'know."

"How long was he in the army for?"

"A few years."

"He was a regular, was he?"

"Yes, 'e must 'ave been in there a good few years. 'e was almost coming out when I met 'im, you see."

"What market does he go to?"

"Up to Covent Garden . . . get the veg, then he sells them down in the Walk, you see."

"What part of Lambeth do you live?"

"One of the roads."

"What's the road called?"

"Cutts Walk."

"I see, what's the number? Do you know the number?"

"Oh yes, fir'y-free."

"33 Cutts Walk, Lambeth."

"Yus, yus. Nice little place, y'know."

"This is 1833, is it?"

"Fir'y-free? . . . eighteen fir'y-free? . . . oh yes, yers, oh must be I should think, yers." (Patronizingly.)

"Haven't got any children yet?"

"No, no, no children."

"Who's the king?"

"King? . . . there's a Queen." (Quick and decisive.)

"Who is the Queen?"

"Queen Victoria."

"How long has she been Queen?"

"Oh, Gawd knows!"

"A long time or not so long?"

"Not long . . . I think."

"She's all right is she?"

"Oh, yers."

"How about the Prime Minister? Who's the Prime Minister?"

"Oh crikey! I don't know prime ministers. Wish I'd learned to read."

"Can't you read?"

"Oh no."

"It's not necessary is it? [Reassuringly.] Can you write a bit?"

"Well, I 'ave to ask people everythink. Write? Oh no. I can put a cross!"

"Is that all you can do?"

"Yes."

"How about Harry? Can he read and write?"

"No, 'e puts a cross, too."

"Does he?"

"M . . . m."

"I want you to go forward in time, Liza. Liza Bloggs, I want you to forward in time another ten years . . . another ten years . . . and you are now forty. Liza Bloggs, go forward to the time when you were forty. This is the year 1843 and you're forty, Liza Bloggs. How old are you, Liza?"

"I'm for'y now."

"In good health?"

"Oh yes, I always 'ad pretty good 'ealth, y'know. Gettin' a bit fat o'course."

"How's Harry?"

"Harry? Oh, he's very well. Doing very well on the business too . . . yes."

"Still in the same business?"

"Oh, 'e don't know nothin' but 'is veg."

"And where do you live now?"

"We're still at fir'y-free."

"You are?"

"Yers."

"Any children?"

"No. It's a pity, ain't it. I would have loved some kids, but we just didn't 'ave none."

"I want you to go forward in time another ten years, Liza Bloggs [she took a deep breath] and you are now fifty. Liza Bloggs, you are now fifty. [She suddenly became very still.] How old you are, Liza? [No reply. I waited a few moments and repeated the question.] How old are you, Liza? . . . fifty years after you were born. [Still no reply.] Go back, Liza, to when you were forty-five, Liza Bloggs. Liza Bloggs, you are now forty-five, Liza. You are now forty-five. [She took a deep breath.] How old are you, Liza?"

"I'm for'y-five."

"Are you in good health?"

"Yes, but I do get this pain in my chest. I think it must be indigestion, but ooh, I get this pain in my chest!"

"How long have you been getting it, dear?"

"Well, I suppose a long time, on and off you know. I don't know quite 'ow long. Good while."

"Putting on weight still?"

"I'm afraid so, but y'see I do like me old glass of stout. That's what it is."

"How's Harry?"

"Oh, 'e's fine me old 'arry, bless 'is old 'eart."

"How old is he?"

"Forty-five? . . . er, forty-five? [Contemplating her own age.] 'arry will be about fifty now."

"Didn't have any children, did you?"

"No, I'm really very sorry about that. I am sorry about that."

"Liza, go forward in time two years, will you. Go forward in time, Liza Bloggs, to when you were forty-seven. Go forward in time, Liza, to when you were forty-seven. How old are you, Liza?"

"I'm forty-seven." (She seemed to have difficulty in breathing.)

"What's wrong, dear?"

"Me pain's bad . . . me pain's very bad!"

"How about a doctor?"

"Oh yes, I 'ad a doctor."

"What did you say?"

"Oh, 'e give me some pills and 'e gave me some . . . [she gasped a little] . . . funny little things to break and sniff up me nose."

"When do you get the pain? What brings on the pain, Liza?"

"Oh, seems to me when I come up the stairs."

"What did he tell you to do when the pain comes on?"

"He says I mustn't lay down. I 'ave to be propped up and oh, I 'ave to break one of these things and sniff. [The treatment for the alleviation of angina pectoris, the symptoms of which she was describing, used to be the inhalation of the drug amyl nitrite.] Then I catches me breath sharp and the pain begins to go away."? Her breathing was more laboured.)

"And then?"

"And then I 'ave to rest after that."

"Harry good to you?"

"Ah, 'arry's ever so good to me, yes."

"Tell me, when you were very young, when you were about fifteen, what colour was your hair?" (I suddenly remembered a physician once telling me how impressed he had been by the number of red-headed girls who developed angina pectoris later in life. He claimed this was only his observation, but I thought it worth the question.)

"They used to call me old ginger-knob!"

"Still ginger, is it?"

"No, it's dark now . . . sort of dark brown, y'know."

"Liza, I want you to go forward in time to the day that you

died. Liza Bloggs, I want you to go forward in time to the day
that you died. Go forward in time to the day that you died.
How old are you today?''

"I . . . I can't seem to get my breath very well today . . . no.''
(Her breathing was very laboured.)

"Doctor been?''

"Yes . . . [gasping] . . . he's been this morning . . . and he's
coming again tonight.''

"What's his name?''

"Just . . . just a minute . . . [she was struggling for
breath] . . . Doctor Levy.''

"Doctor Levy?''

"Yes.''

"Nice man?''

"Oh . . . very kind . . . very kind . . . yes . . . [gasping] . . . oh
yes.''

"Do you think you're going to get better soon?''

"I don't feel . . . as though I am . . . I . . . oh dear!''
[She was very distressed by now as she struggled more and
more for breath. She was obviously in a very advanced state of
cardiac failure.] . . . oh dear . . . it's . . . awful hard . . . to
breathe . . .'' (Gasping desperately.)

"Go forward, Liza. Go forward, Liza. You will understand
me and you will hear me. [She was struggling for each
breath.] Go forward to a few minutes after you died. Now you
will feel peaceful and well. [Her gasping stopped.] But go
forward and you will understand me. You will be able to
answer me. Go forward to a few minutes after you died and
tell me of your experiences. You will be able to answer me,
Liza. Tell me, Liza, what happened soon after you died? You
will be able to answer me. What happened? What happened,
Liza? [She took her usual deep breath of regression.] Can you
tell me?''

"Cold . . .'' (She whispered.)

"Cold?''

"Ever . . . so . . . cold.''

"Do you see anyone?''

(She shook her head, "no" . . .)

"No? All right, dear. All right, dear.''

My attempt to follow Liza into the 'astral planes' had not

met with success. Nevertheless, I was delighted with the Liza recording that I had made. Joan and Bill were spellbound. To have discovered two totally different personalities in just two sessions surpassed my wildest expectations. I knew from previous experience that Peggy Bailey would be none the worse for her regression. Why should she when she had come out of the Sally Barnes regression so well only a few weeks previously? So it was with a certain sense of confidence that I decided to try and relocate Sally before bringing her back to the present time. I quote from the original tape-recording made at the time:

"And now I want you to go back in time. You're going back in time a long way. You're going back in time, going back, back, back. Back in time to the time when you were someone else on this earth. To the time when you were someone else on this earth. To the time when you were Sally Barnes. Going back to the time when you were Sally Barnes. And today Sally Barnes it is your thirtieth birthday. Today Sally Barnes it is your thirtieth birthday. It is your thirtieth birthday and you feel comfortable and well. This, Sally Barnes, is your thirtieth birthday, thirtieth birthday, thirtieth birthday. Sally Barnes, it is your thirtieth birthday and the year is 1746. It's 1746. Hello Sally! [a pause] How old are you, Sally? [a pause] You are thirty today. How old are you, Sally? [She took a deep breath – no reply yet.] How old are you?"

"Oim thirty." (Immediately the rich Devon accent of Sally.)

"What sort of day is it?"

"Oh, it's a foin day."

"How's Sam?"

"Oh, he's jes' foin, thank you."

"Is he?"

"Oh yes."

"What's he doing this time of the year?"

"Oh, hay-making and things, y'know."

"Well, it's June, isn't it. June the fourth?"

"Oh yes."

"How are you going to spend your birthday?"

"Oh, I don't know. I'll go for a little walk, I guess. I'll go down to the river for a while, I think."

"How far is it to the river?"

"Oh, jest a little ways."

This confirmed Peggy's ability to produce either Sally or Liza on request. I had established that Sally and Liza were always there to be re-visited, each with her own personality, characteristics, mannerisms and experiences. In my own time I could get to know them well. This I intended to do.

Peggy Bailey returned home with her husband after that session, once again her usual cheerful self; knowing little and caring less about what had happened on the hypnosis couch.

Let us briefly reconsider the information obtained so far. Sally Fraser was born around 1716 and died about 1783. After a gap of twenty years Liza was born in approximately 1803 and she died in 1850. Peggy Bailey was born in 1921, giving a gap of about seventy years. I wondered if there was another 'life' which would conveniently fill this period. On the assumption that there was a 'resting period' of about twenty years between each incarnation this would only give a life span of thirty years or even less for any incarnation during this time. My calculations might not be all that accurate but they could not be very wrong. Supposing she were reborn again twenty years after Liza's death (that is around 1870) and went on to enjoy ripe old age of three score years and ten or more, then there would be an overlap with Peggy's birth in 1921 with obvious implications. Perhaps there was no incarnation between Liza and Peggy. These thoughts tormented me until the next session at which I decided to investigate the possible hidden mysteries locked away in Peggy Bailey's deep psychic memory at the turn of the twentieth century.

6

Assessment and Discussion II

When Leonard Wilder next put Peggy Bailey into a deep trance, regressed her to her own childhood and then asked her to go back in time to when she was someone else on this earth, she immediately responded with the name 'Liza', in a broad cockney accent.

The immediate acceptance by the hypnotist of a further personality might be considered suspect by some disinterested observers. Almost too ready to accept the 'lucky break', one has to ask oneself whether the hypnotist had unconsciously 'willed' another 'personality' to manifest; providing this is possible, and who can say?

The brain is a very complicated piece of apparatus, so complicated in fact that when, during the course of some world-wide tests in extra-sensory perception and in particular in telepathy, I asked some American scientists whether it was likely that a machine would ever be manufactured that would duplicate the functions of the human brain, I was told that it was hardly likely. Why? Because the human brain is so complicated that some ten billion electronic tubes would be necessary to duplicate its functions. Furthermore, I was told, so clumsy would such an artificial brain be in comparison with the human brain that it would be likely to require all the electricity generated by the Niagara Falls for power and, in addition, it would need a similar volume of power to cool it.

Where, then, did 'Liza' originate? Was she a figment of the hypnotist's imagination, transmitted unconsciously to the subject? Was she a fictional character whom Peggy Bailey had read about long ago and who was now returning from the depths of Peggy's unconscious memory? Was her genesis in the unconscious imagination of the subject? Was she the result of telepathic communication from some other source, transmitted to the hypnotized subject? Or could she be a genuine previous life of Peggy Bailey? In many psychic experiments it is less easy to accept a complicated rational explanation that is acceptable to science than to believe in a psychic explanation.

To accept reincarnation presupposes acceptance of an after-life for if we do not survive death, then reincarnation cannot be. Converseley if we accept 'Liza' as a regression to a previous life of Peggy Bailey, we accept survival of something after the death of the physical body. Few scientists accept that there is scientific proof of survival and therefore they prefer to accept a physical explanation for so-called regression, no matter how complicated and involved that explanation may be.

Furthermore the adherents of reincarnation – and there are many, perhaps the majority of mankind – maintain that the 'soul' or essential component of a human being is reborn on earth again and again to redeem the debts of karma: the sins accumulated during previous lives. Karma is the Eastern teaching of the law of cause and effect – "whatsoever a man soweth, that shall he also reap". To the scientist all the evidence of biology, anthropology and paleontology suggests that man in essence is an animal, so the necessary tenets of reincarnation are not acceptable.

Yet the whole idea that man is merely an animal is a materialistic concept, while reincarnation and the doctrine of karma are based on the idea that man is essentially spiritual, the complicated system of karma having been promulgated to explain away the inequalities of man. In accepting a spiritual philosophy in these difficult regions, it is presupposed that man is something more than a product of his animal instincts and drives. Thus there are two opposing viewpoints and each person must decide for himself which he chooses. It may be that the apparent regressions of Peggy Bailey will make it easier for some people to make up their minds.

There is another problem, and a not uncommon one, that is a scientific fact and for which it is difficult to suggest an easier, more straightforward and more logical explanation than reincarnation; a problem that is sometimes referred to as 'overshadowing'. It covers the thousands of apparently inexplicable examples of dual personality and the conscious memory of previous lives by some people.

Scholars still discuss how Pythagoras, the Greek philosopher, could have deceived himself, consciously or unconsciously, with memories of past lives, including his own name in a previous existence, and he partially verified one incarnation by visiting the scene of a battle he had taken part in as a soldier in another life and finding the very shield he had used. There have been similar cases in every age, and in our own time many people have claimed that they have consciously known that they have lived before.

In 1972 an Ilford woman and her mother believed that she was the reincarnation of her great-grandmother. When she was less than two years old, she chatted away about the time when she had been a big girl and lived on a farm and had lots of animals and many sons, one of whom was called Nicholas. This woman's grandfather's name was Nicholas.

An inhabitant of Crouch End has remembered, as long as she can recall, being an Italian painter in a previous existence, and on her first visit to Venice she found all the streets and the buildings familiar. Finding her way without difficulty in a city she had not previously visited in this life, she felt very strongly that she had known the place before, long ago.

An Italian housewife states that she lived before in France as Jeanne de la Platière and was guillotined in 1793, and although she does not know French she can recite in full her 'Appeal to Posterity' in the original French.

An American clerk, nineteen-year-old Josephine Straker, stated in 1972 that she lived before as a nurse with Florence Nightingale at the time of the Crimean War, and she has always known this. She so minutely described officers who visited front-line hospitals that they were identified as Lord Raglan, the British commander, and his aides.

A London designer has always believed that he was once a Scotsman named Angus MacCallum who died in 1490 as a result of an arrow wound. He wrote a story which he thought was pure invention and later discovered that all the people he had 'invented' had really lived five hundred years before.

Dual personality is a separate but related mystery that

In 1745 the Foundling Hospital was built in Guilford Street and 600 children were removed from the premises in Hatton Garden. Here, where the expenses of the establishment were at one period more than five times the amount of the income, a basket was hung at the gate in which children could be deposited and a bell rung to advise the officers in attendance. On the first day at Guilford Street, 2 June 1756, 117 children were so received; and in three years 14,934 children were received, 10,389 of whom died. In 1926 the Foundling Hospital left Bloomsbury for temporary quarters at Redhill, Surrey, and in 1935 moved to Berkhamsted. If Liza was received at the 'Foundlings' soon after her birth in 1803, this would have been, therefore, at Guilford Street, Russell Square, Bloomsbury, and it is hard to see any connection with Millbank, Westminster. On the other hand Liza might well have been very ignorant about London and, anxious to supply a district when asked to do so, gave in reply the first area she thought of. It is likely that the Millbank area would be mentioned in the household of a Lord of the realm, not only because of its prison, but also on account of its gardens, wharves and proximity to superior houses.

One final thought on this curiously inaccurate siting of the Foundling Hospital. Millbank was once the name of what is now Grosvenor Road. Could Liza, in her ignorance and anxiety to give *some* information, have confused Guilford with Grosvenor and correctly identified the latter with Millbank? But let us return from such flights of fancy to Liza and her actual words.

She describes Piccadilly. "Ooh, big 'ouses, y'know ... one big 'ouse, bit of green, another big house, bit more green ... you know ..." Not particularly evocative and expressive perhaps, and yet how very descriptive for an untutored person. It really is quite a good description – and very economical in adjectives!

Again and again one is struck by the staggering authenticity of the material that came through. It is so exactly what one would expect from a Victorian girl, slaving away below stairs: is there simply too much that rings true for it to be all false? Is this not a cockney speaking? Consider the answers to these questions:

"Ever been out of London?"

"Cor no! 'course I ain't."

"How about school? Ever go to school?"

"Ah, they used to teach us a few things."

Have you been a long time with Mrs Bates?"

"No . . . no, not very long, but blimey it don't 'arf seem a long time. Clips me round the ear she does, somethink shocking . . ."

"Have you got another name?"

"Well, I s'pose I must have, but I'm only ever called Liza . . suits them."

"What do you do when you're not working?"

"Cor crikey, I'm always working!"

However one may fault that part of Peggy Bailey that calls itself Liza, it is not authenticity of characterization.

At first sight "Mr blooming Jenkins" (the butler) smacks of artificiality and it is possible that this is exactly what 'he' is. Long an accepted name for a butler in fiction, it may well have been the name by which the butler in the Frobisher household was known to the kitchen staff – in derision; perhaps the only name by which they knew him. So many 'maybes', 'buts' and 'perhapses'. . . !

Having established a very believable – and likable – character in Liza, the thirteen-year-old skivvy of all work, it is interesting, to say the least, to see the character attempt a completely new diction and outlook by becoming the personal maid of the lady of the house. Again one is inclined to surmise that this is simply not a course one is likely to have chosen in the given circumstances; more likely surely to have sought to have verified the cockney maid instead of complicating matters by having her mistress improve her education with the inevitable result of a mixture of artificiality and lapses into cockney slang.

The complete indifference to her age is very typical of Liza's type of girl at that time, but again, is this something that Peggy Bailey would have known, or Leonard Wilder, and if not, then whence came the knowledge?

Eager to substantiate or denounce matters of fact that are revealed in such experiments I pounced on two items that 'Liza' mentioned: the uniform ("little round 'at, blue trousers and nice red jacket") at Wellington Barracks in 1833 and the address, Cutts Walk.

On the question of the uniform I wrote to Wellington Barracks asking whether any uniform in use by soldiers at the Barracks about 1830 consisted of a little round hat, blue trousers and red jacket. I received a reply from Major J. Hughes, M.B.E, Regimental Headquarters, Scots Guards, Bloomsbury Court, and the substance of his letter was contained in the sentence: "The uniform you describe could well be that of one of the Guards Regiments." It was the kind of reply that made me anxious to have 'Liza' asked more about 'Harry Bloggs'.

Somewhat to my surprise I was unable to trace a thoroughfare with the name Cutts Walk, although The Cut runs between Blackfriars Road and Waterloo Road in Lambeth, a road that was originally known as New Cut. In fact it became a street within the memory of John Timbs, author of the monumental *Curiosities of London* first published in 1855. Timbs writes of "low-lying fields, with a large windmill, east of the raised roadway" and it seems more than possible that there was an alleyway, byway or short cut in the locality that was known (perhaps unofficially) so descriptively as Cutts Walk; and it must have been of some length since 'Liza' gave the number of her house as 33. In common with so much that has been investigated in this case, the conclusion on the description of the uniform and the road, Cutts Walk, must be "Unproven" – so far.

Confusion continued when Liza was questioned about the reigning monarch. The year was 1833 and the question was "Who's the king?" The correct answer would have been William IV, the sailor king, who reigned from 1765 to 1837 when Queen Victoria began her "glorious reign". Yet Liza, born in the reign of William IV and living her whole life (up to that time) under his rule, replied "quick and decisive": "King? there is a Queen." A second later when asked which queen: "Queen Victoria." Asked how long she had been queen, Liza replied, "Oh, Gawd knows!" And she seemed to know even less about the prime ministers of the day, but then of course she couldn't read, as she tactfully reminds the hynotist in the same breath. It is perhaps worth mentioning here although it merely adds to the confusion, that this exchange hampers the hypothesis of role-taking and also the possibility of obtaining information telepathically from the hypnotist. In role-taking such information is much more likely to have been correct and in any telepathic communication with Leonard Wilder it would certainly have been correct.

So what are we to make of this simple maidservant not even knowing the name of the reigning monarch? No further explanation is required, I suggest, than to recall that only thirty years ago, immediately after the Second World War, it was estimated that half the world's population was illiterate and we are dealing with 1833, over 140 years ago. On the other hand 'true recall' does sometimes include mistakes.

The "funny little pills to break up and sniff up me nose" described by Liza is clearly not the present-day treatment (as might have been expected) for angina pectoris, which seems to be the complaint that 'Liza' suffers from, for she exactly describes the archaic treatment *at that time*.

'Doctor Levy' was my next target and I tried, first of all, The Medical Society of London. Unfortunately their records are not comprehensive and are, I learned, virtually restricted to personalities who have been members of that Society. The Registrar most kindly examined the available records for the appropriate years but was unable to trace that a Dr Levy or Levi was a Fellow of the Society.

I next approached the Royal Society of Medicine where I asked, as I had the Medical Society of London, whether they could trace in their records a Doctor Levy (the spelling might be different) who had apparently practised in 1850 in the Lambeth area. The Librarian replied (4 June 1974): "I cannot trace a Dr Levy in the Lambeth area about 1850 but since you say you are unsure of the spelling I wondered if the name might have been Lever?" Mr Wade, the Librarian, was good enough to send me copies of *The London and Provincial Medical Directory* 1850 and *The Lancet* 1859, Volume 1, Number 75, showing that there was a Dr J.C.W. Lever associated with the Lambeth area at the time in question.

In the *London and Provincial Medical Directory* his address is given as 12 Wellington Street, Southwark, and he is described as a lecturer on midwifery at Guy's Hospital and author of *Organic Diseases of the Uterus*.

The mention in *The Lancet* for 15 January 1859 is in fact an obituary notice and the considerable account of his life and work leave little doubt that he *could* have been the doctor referred to by Liza as attending her about 1850. Dr J.C.W. Lever started as a general practitioner in Bridgehouse Place, Newington Causeway, in 1834. In 1842 he was appointed assistant to Dr Ashwell as physician-accoucheur and lecturer at Guy's Hospital and he then moved to Wellington Street, London Bridge. The following year he was awarded the Fothergillian gold medal for his essay on the organic diseases of the uterus. In 1845, on Dr Ashwell's retirement from Guy's Hospital, Dr Lever was appointed lecturer in midwifery and physician-accoucheur to the institute, a Dr Oldham sharing with him the honours and labours of that position.

Dr Lever was first married in 1836 and had six children by his wife who died in 1849. He married a second time in 1851 and was survived by his second wife and a son and a daughter of the marriage.

Was this the 'Doctor Levy' known to Liza? I made a note to arrange for Leonard Wilder to ask one or two questions in an attempt to settle the matter one way or the other at a future session with Peggy Bailey.

7
Alice

Sixth of June, 1958, and the days were now almost at their longest, with warm, pleasant, scented evenings. Sundays should have been spent lazing up on Hampstead Heath, relaxing after the week's confinement in a dental surgery. But curiosity and the compulsion to further explore the mystery of possible reincarnation cast such sentiments aside. The following Sunday afternoon found the four 'adventurers' once again in the half-lit room where we had first met Sally Fraser and Liza Bloggs.

Peggy, as usual, asked no questions but quietly accepted my experiments as being bona fide. Soon she was lying on the couch in deep trance. I decided to aim at just after the year 1900 and try to see what Peggy might produce. I quote from the recordings:

"It is now 1903. It is now 1903. Now tell me where you are. Tell me what you can see about you. [She took a deep breath.] Yes? [No reply.] Can you see anything? What can you see? Tell me. You will be able to tell me. [Another deep breath.] You will. You can do it. [A deep breath.] Are you on the earth? [She nodded.] You are. Are you in the spirit world? [She shook her head.] You're not. Are you a person? [She nodded again.] You are. Well, tell me what is your name? [She was still taking deep breaths as though the mists were thinning and she was experiencing a slow re-awakening.] Do you know? Will it help you if you go forward in time? [She shook her head.] Or back? [She shook her head again.] You think you can tell me what you are, as you are now? [She nodded.] 1903? [Another nod.] Good. Are you very young? [She nodded. I wondered how young as so far the only communication had been either a nodding or shaking of her head. I felt impatient to make verbal contact. Justifiably so, I'm sure.] How young? Tell me roughly your age. [She was trying to form words.] Are you older than ten, or younger? Are you older or younger?"

"Young . . . young . . . younger." (A gradual breakthrough and immediately the voice of a child.)

"That's right, younger than ten. You see, you're speaking." (Encouragingly.)

"Yes."

"Good. Now, how old are you?"

(She paused.)

"I'm s . ., I'm six."

"You're six. What's your name, dear?"

"Six."

"Good." (I felt that she was still trying to orientate herself.)

"Alice."

"Alice. Alice what?"

"Just Alice." (Quietly spoken with a good, cultured accent. I had not been disappointed. So here was that other 'life' appearing just where I had expected! I felt like an astronomer who, having predicted a new planet and then looked through his telescope, had found it as anticipated.)

"I see. Where do you live, Alice?"

"In a big house."

"Where?"

(She was slow in answering.)

"In London."

"In London. What part of London, dear?"

"In . . . near St James's Park."

"I see. And have you a mummy and daddy?"

"Yes, I have a nanny."

"You have a nanny?"

"Yes."

"And any brothers or sisters? [She breathed deeply, but it was more like a sigh.] Have you, Alice? [She did not reply. This was no happy, carefree child of six. Although not unintelligent, she was not particularly forthcoming. I sensed that all was not quite normal.] Alice, I want you to go forward in time to your tenth birthday. Alice, go forward in time to your tenth birthday. Today, Alice, you are ten. Today, Alice, you are ten. How old are you, Alice?"

"I'm ten." (Quietly and respectfully.)

"That's right. Now Alice, what is your second name, Alice?"

"I'm just Alice." (Subdued.)

"And have you a mummy and a daddy?"

"Oh yes, oh yes, I have."

"And what does your daddy do?"

"He rides in a big carriage."

"And do you go to school?"

"Oh no, someone comes to me."

"Do you have a governess?"

"Yes." (Still quietly polite.)

"And where do you live?"

"By St James's Park."

"And . . . you have any brothers and sisters?"

"No, no." (I was concerned by her rather pathetic attitude, which was so very different to little Liza at almost the same age. There was an underlying sadness in her voice.)

"I want you to go forward in time now, little Alice. I want you to go forward in time, I want you to go forward in time, Alice, to your fifteenth birthday, to your fifteenth birthday and the year is 1912. Alice it is now 1912 and I want you to go forward to your fifteenth birthday. How old are you, Alice?"

"I'm fifteen." (Her voice was maturing and cultured. I was getting troubled by the thought that Peggy was born in 1921. We now had young Alice aged fifteen in 1912. At the time of Peggy's birth, Alice would only be twenty-four!)

"And what do you do? Are you still studying? Do you still have a governess?"

"Yes. I have a tutor also." (I detected the slightest trace of a Scottish inflection in her answer. This was the only noticeable time. Perhaps she had acquired it from a parent or a member of the staff. I overlooked the chance of following this up.)

"And what is your second name, Alice?"

"I'm just Alice."

"I see. And where do you live, Alice?"

"Near St James's Park."

"Can you give me the address?"

"No, because I don't go out very often."

"Why not?"

"I don't walk very well."

"Why is that, dear? Would you tell me?"

"Well, my legs don't move."

"Oh, I see. Did you have an illness as a little girl?"

"I don't ever remember walking."

"Oh, I see. And what does your father do, dear?"

"He's a banker."

"Where? What bank? Do you know?"

"Oh no. In the Strand somewhere, I think."

"You come from a very good family, of course?"

"Well, it depends what you call good." (With complete modesty.)

"Right Alice, I want you to go forward a little in time. I want you to go forward a little in time. I want you to go forward a little in time and now, today is your twentieth birthday. Today you are twenty, and it is 1919. [She took a deep breath.] Today you are twenty. How old are you, Alice?"

"I'm twenty." (As with Sally and Liza, her character was becoming more established as I progressed her. With Alice it was polite, refined and cultured.)

"And are you in good health?" (There were only two years now before Peggy's birth!)

"Well, I don't know about good. I suppose I am. I get rather bored just being in all the time."

"And you're still not able to walk?"

"Oh no. I don't suppose I ever shall."

"Why is that?"

"Well, it's something to do with my legs."

"And apart from your legs, what is the rest of your health like?"

"Oh, I get very depressed, you know."

"But you're able to use your arms, are you?"

"Oh yes, I do my embroidery."

"And what other names have you other than Alice?"

"I'm just Alice." (This was positively frustrating. I was just not able to get an answer to this question. Were she role-taking, then the invention of a name would have presented no problem.)

"I see. I want you to go forward in time. I want you to go forward in time to your twenty-fifth birday, Alice. I want you to go forward in time to your twenty-fifth birthday and the year is 1924. [My hand holding the microphone was trembling.

Would Alice's lifetime overlap with Peggy's?] This is your
twenty-fifth birthday and the year is 1924. How old are you
today?" [No breath! I waited for a few moments. No answer!] I
want you to go back in time, Alice, to the day before you died.
Alice, I want you to go back in time to the day before you died.
[A breath.] You are going back in time to the day before you
died, Alice. [A deep breath.] How are you, Alice, today? [No
immediate reply.] Can you answer me?"

"I . . . I think I can . . . just."

"What's wrong, dear? Tell me."

"It's . . . something to do with my legs and it's affecting me
all over."

"And how old are you?"

"I'll soon be twenty-two." (In which case she was still
twenty-one and the year would be 1920. If this were an
authentic reincarnation and the dates were accurate, then
Peggy's rebirth as herself would have occurred within a year.
This would result in a very short 'resting period'.)

"You'll soon be twenty-two."

"Yes."

"What is the date of your birthday? What day and month
were you born?"

"I don't know. They . . . they just told me how old I was."

"And what is the year? Do you know?"

"Oh, I can't think . . . I . . . oh dear, I'm afraid I don't feel
very well." (She was completely dignified, showing no
outward sign of physical distress.)

"All right, dear. Thank you, Alice. Thank you."

I had the uneasy feeling throughout this recording that
although Alice was conducting herself correctly and politely
there was a profound reluctance to relate her experiences and
sentiments. I sensed an aura of unfulfilment and deep
frustration, as of an enforced waiting for time to take its
inevitable course. Perhaps that was why this sad girl, Alice,
was the very last 'life' to present itself. I terminated the
interrogations, brought her back to the present as Peggy, and
woke her up.

Another week to wait, but in due course the weekend
arrived and with it time for further investigation. This time I
did not give Peggy's subconscious mind the chance to choose
which 'life' to present. After the somewhat unproductive

session with Alice the week before, I indicated to Peggy, once again hypnotized and in deep trance, the precise year to which I wanted her to regress. I quote:

". . . 1912 and you are now someone. Who are you? 1912. [A pause. A breath.] Yes?"

"I'm Alice." (Almost surprised.)

"Yes, you're Alice. Yes, you're Alice. How old are you, Alice? It's 1912."

"I'm . . . er . . . er."

"Well, approximately."

"I'm eighteen."

"You're eighteen. I thought you'd be about fifteen but we're not far out, are we?"

"No."

"No. Tell me, Alice, how do you spend your time? What do you do?"

"Oh, I read a great deal."

"What do you read?"

"Oh, I think pretty well everything."

"What books do you like reading?"

"I like to read about the birds and the flowers."

"Yes."

"And novels."

"What novels have you read?"

"Oh well, several. I read *The Blue Lagoon*."

"Oh really, who wrote that? Who's the author? Do you know?"

"I think H. de Vere Stacpoole."

"Oh I see. What's it about?"

"Oh, some children on a desert island."

"You read that recently, did you?"

"Well, amongst others. Really, I wasn't supposed to read it."

"Really?"

"Father didn't want me to. He said it isn't very nice."

"Isn't it?"

"Well, I suppose it depends on one's outlook, really."

"M . . . m. Do you think he's rather Victorian?"

"Well you see, me being at home, I think he sort of likes to treasure me a little."

"Do you like that?"

"Well, yes I do. He's all I have, you see." (I assumed from that remark that she had no mother.)

"When did your mother die?"

"Oh, when I was born."

"And you have no brothers or sisters?"

"Oh no. I wish I had."

"Now, your father's name is . . .?"

"Sir George."

"Your father's name is Sir George."

"Oh, yes."

"Sir George what?"

"Browning."

"Sir George Browning, is it?"

"Yes."

"And you're the Hon. Alice Browning, are you?"

"Well, I'm just called Miss Alice."

"I see. And has he been in the army at all when he was a young man? Do you know?"

"Oh yes, I think he was in India at some time."

"What rank was he?"

"Oh, I believe he was a colonel."

"He was a colonel was he? A full colonel?"

"Yes."

"He was a full colonel. And have you any aunts or uncles?"

"We have, you know, but they seem to leave him awfully much alone. I don't know why."

"And what bank does he work at?"

"The bank is in the Strand."

"Do you know which bank it is? Is it the bank of . . .?"

"No, he just goes to the bank."

"And what is his work there? Do you know?"

"Well, he just looks after it, you see."

"Oh, I see. Mm."

"I suppose you would call him the manager or something."

"I see. What other books have you read recently?"

"Well, I always read my favourite, you know. That's *Alice in Wonderland*."

"Why do you like *Alice in Wonderland*?"

"Oh, it's very amusing."

"Is it because your name is Alice?"

"No, I think it's because I see it and it sort of takes me away somewhere."

"Does it?"

"Oh yes, and it's very amusing."

"Who wrote it?"

"Oh, Lewis Carroll, everyone knows Lewis Carroll wrote that."

"That his real name?"

"I presume so."

"Well, it isn't really."

"Oh?"

"It isn't really. Lewis Carroll was a mathematician and that was the only novel he ever wrote." (This is incorrect. Lewis Carroll, real name Charles Lutwidge Dodgson, although essentially a mathematician, did write a few other fanciful children's stories.)

"Is that so? That's rather a pity, you know."

"Is it?"

"Oh yes. Wouldn't it have been interesting if he had written some other books?" (In retrospect, I am surprised that she hadn't heard of *Alice Through the Looking Glass*.)

"What part of the book do you like best?"

"I think where the baby turns into a pig." (Her serious nature relaxed a little.)

"You liked that bit, did you?"

"I think that's awfully funny." (The slightest suggestion of her own voice as Peggy crept in at this point. This had certainly not occurred with Sally or Liza.)

"That's the bit they call 'Pig and Pepper', isn't it?" (She chuckled at that remark.)

"Yes, well it was."

"And what other books do you like reading?"

"Ooh, I just read anything, really. We have sort of a glossy sort of a thin paper coloured book, which tells all the things that are going on in Society."

"Yes, what's the name of this book?"

"Oh dear, I just pick it up and look, you know."

"Tell me, who is the King?"

"The King?"

"Yes."

"Now?"

"Yes."

"Oh, George."

"King George?"

"Yes."

"How long has he been King?"

"Some time. Oh yes, some time." (King George V came to the throne in 1910.)

"Was he King when you were a very small, little girl? When you were about six or seven was he, do you think?"

"Oh no, there was another King then."

"Who was that?"

"I think it was King Edward."

"Quite right, it was. Yes. What is your address? If I wanted to find your house, if I was going to visit you, how would I find your house if there was no one to ask in the street?"

"Well, there's a carriage step outside with a statue of a little black boy."

"Really?" (I jumped at this piece of information. So far the establishment of Alice's personality had been rather laborious compared with Sally or Liza. This is not exactly surprising, though, with someone who was confined to her home.)

"Yes."

"And supposing I were coming, what part of London would I have to come to?"

"You have to come to the edge of St James's Park."

"Which edge?"

"The edge nearest to Green Park."

"I see, and then what would I do?"

"The house overlooks the park."

"Yes, and I'd look for this statue of a little black boy."

"Well, I expect if you asked, anyone could tell you where Sir George's house was."

"If there was no one to ask, how would I find it?"

"But there would be someone. There's always someone?"

"Yes, I suppose there would. Have you many servants in the house?"

"No, I have my governess, you see, and she's a governess and nurse."

"What's her name?"

"Celia."

"Celia what?"

"I just call her Celia."

"Where does she live?"

"Oh, she lives with us." (She sounded surprised that I had not taken it for granted.)

"She lives with you, does she?"

"Oh yes."

"Does er . . . Celia is more or less full time with you, is she? She's a companion as well, is she?"

"Oh yes."

"And does she teach you lots of things? She's obviously given you a good education. You're well spoken."

"Well, do you think so?" (Slightly amused.)

"I do indeed, yes. What does she teach you?"

"Just a little bit of everything, I suppose. She taught me my writing. She helps me with the reading, needlework . . ."

"Yes?"

". . . painting . . ."

"Yes?"

". . . music."

"Yes. Do you play any instrument?"

"Oh no, I'm supposed to sing but really I think I have a dreadful voice."

"I see. And she's taught you languages, has she, little bits of languages?"

"No, I didn't want to learn languages because I knew I would never go anywhere."

"I see. Well, thank you very much. And how about your father? When he has his holidays does he go away and take you with him or does he go away for a short holiday by himself?"

"Oh, he goes away. I think he goes away with some other gentleman that he knows."

"Where does he go?"

"I don't know, really. He just comes and spends a day with me and then goes away."

"And do you ever go out very much?"

"Oh no. I'm pushed to the window and the windows are opened and I can look out over the park."

"But you sometimes go through the park, do you? Are you pushed through the park?"

"No. I don't like to go out."

"Why is that, Alice?"

"Oh, I think people would look at me."

"Have you never been able to walk?"

"Oh no. I don't remember if I have."

"And have they tried to do anything for you?"

"Oh yes, [with a sigh] yes."

"What have they tried to do?"

"They've tried to move my legs about. They've prodded me and . . ."

"Who attends you?"

"Oh, various doctors have been and gone, you know."

"Mm. Can you tell me the name of one of them?"

"Yes. There's one I like very much. He's been coming a long time."

"What's his name, Alice?"

"Sir Harold Somers." (Or "Summers".)

"I see. You like him, do you?"

"Oh yes. He's awfully kind."

"What does he look like?"

"Well now, how shall I describe him? He's not very young."

"Yes."

"He has a little beard."

"Yes."

"And a moustache."

"Yes."

"And very nice blue eyes that crinkle at the corners."

"Oh yes. Is he very tall?"

"Oh yes. He's a large man."

"He is? How old do you think he is?"

"Well, I suppose . . . oh . . . I don't know. I suppose about fifty."

"I see. Alice, I want you to go forward in time. I want you to go forward in time just a few years to the time that you were lying very ill and dying [deep breath]. I want you to go forward in time to the time that you were lying very ill and dying. And you will understand me and you will answer me and you will go beyond death to the time that you were reunited with your mother, and you will describe all these events to me. And you're just on the verge of dying now. Just a few minutes before you died. And you will be able to answer me [deep breath] although at the time you were not able to say very much. You will be able to describe to me what happened and also tell me about your feelings and sentiments. How do you feel?"

"Very, very tired . . . very tired."

"Just tired and nothing else? No pain?"

"No, just tired." (Quiet and composed.)

"Where are you, Alice?"

"I'm lying in my bed."

"And is there anyone with you?"

"Oh yes, my poor Papa. He's . . . he's so very sad, my poor Papa."

"Why is he sad?"

"He knows I'm going to die. They told him I should."

"Is there nothing they can do?"

"There doesn't seem to be. [Sad and resigned.] I don't think I want to stay."

"Where do you want to go?"

"Away from this body of mine . . . away."

"Then go forward in time to the moment that you left your body. Go forward in time to the moment [deep breath] that you left your body [even deeper breath] and tell me. Tell me of your experiences. How do you feel now, Alice? [A pause.] You will be able to tell me. Tell me the experience of dying. Describe it to me . . . how lovely." (I spoke gently and softly.)

"Oh, quiet now."

"What do you see?"

"Oh! [Surprised and delighted.] I see my mother!"

"Tell me more."

"Oh yes, she's stretching out her hands to me. Oh, she's so pleased to see me, and she's very beautiful. Ah, my mother. I've waited so long to see my mother . . . ah!"

"And then? What happened then?"

"She took me in her arms." (This answer is particularly interesting as Alice answered in the past tense in reply to my question which I phrased in the past tense, possibly due to my excitement at the time.)

"And?"

"She's crying. She's so pleased that she's crying."

"Yes?"

"She said [past tense again for no apparent reason], 'Oh Alice, you've come, my baby. I've waited so long for you. I couldn't wait any longer. Oh, At last'."

"And then?"

"She's put her arm around me."

"And?"

"We're going away." (Very softly.)

"You can walk at last?"

"I am walking! [Amazed and delighted.] I am walking!"

"Is that lovely?"

"Oh, yes."

"Can you still see the people in the room?"

"No."

"You can't. Where are you going with your mother? Tell me."

"I don't know." (In a whisper.)

"You're going with her? You're walking with her?"

"Oh, yes." (Very softly.)

"You will be able to keep on speaking to me and you will be able to tell me everything. Tell me where you are going with her."

"I don't know . . . [a quiet whisper] . . . I don't know." (Almost inaudible.)

"Well, then, go forward a little in time until you are able to tell me your experiences. Just a little in time. [No reply.] You can't? [She shook her head very slowly.] You can't . . ."

She lay very still, breathing quietly and gently, the same signs that I had seen when Sally and Liza had 'died'. I took her pulse. It was steady and normal. Alice had 'died' somewhere between 1916 and 1919. Peggy Bailey had been born in 1921. A short 'resting period' but no overlap. The reincarnation hypothesis was still open for analysis. I returned Peggy to the present and brought her out of hypnosis. Once again she felt well and relaxed and was soon enjoying the Sunday afternoon tea which she had, albeit unknowingly, so richly deserved.

We met again two weeks after the Alice Browning episode

and I attempted to regress her to a time period before Sally
Fraser, but met with no result. Each time she just lay there
quietly on the couch and did not respond. I could hardly say I
was disappointed. With Sally, Liza and Alice on the tapes
there had, indeed, been a fine harvest of regression. Before
returning her to the present I briefly stopped off at 'Sally' to
reconfirm some of the questions I had previously asked her.
When I came to play back the tape I was distressed to find
that due to a fault in the machine it had not recorded.
However, I do remember her reference to "My Beauty", her
dog. She also mentioned two men who helped on the farm as
her husband Sam grew older. These she named as Job, for
whom she had particular affection, and Harry, who did not
seem to have won much of her attention. This is the only
recording that was wasted. I lost no time in treating myself to
a new machine.

Joan and I had planned a touring holiday of the West
Country for the first two weeks of July. We rearranged our
itinerary to enable us to spend a weekend in Exeter. It would
be an excellent opportunity to try and find the location of
Sally Fraser's life in the eighteenth century. Armed with maps
of that part of Devon we set off in my car with a sense of high
anticipation.

8
Assessment and Discussion III

It is perhaps pertinent at this point to recall that the present series of experiments is not the first instance of apparent regression to a previous life under hypnosis. Particularly well known is the Bridey Murphy case and many psychical researchers, reviewers, newspapermen and laymen found *The Search for Bridey Murphy* an intriguing prima facie case for reincarnation; it was even suggested that it was the most important work of its kind to be published this century.

Morey Bernstein, a Colorado businessman, discovered that he possessed the ability to hypnotize. As he experimented he found that certain subjects could recall events in their youth which they had forgotten in their waking life. Having discovered a young married woman, Virginia Burns Tighe (whom Bernstein called 'Ruth Simmons' in the book), to be singularly susceptible to hypnosis, the amateur hypnotist decided to attempt to regress her to a time when she was someone else on earth.

Without difficulty Virginia Tighe seemingly assumed a new personality, Bridey Murphy, who said she had been born at Cork in Ireland in 1798 and had died at Belfast in 1864.

The story that was subsequently unfolded was jumbled and sometimes vague and superficial but small places in Ireland were mentioned that appeared on few maps and she showed a remarkable and accurate feeling for the period in which she was supposed to have lived; and she conversed in what seems to have been genuine Irish brogue.

Bridey spoke of meeting lots of people in the world beyond the grave whom she had known in her life on earth and she described the afterlife as a place of transition where there is no pain, no sleep, no eating and no drinking.

Later, however, some doubt was cast on the authenticity of the affair when it was alleged that Virginia Tighe had had lengthy conversations as a young girl with an Irish woman who had emigrated to America, and the whole Bridey Murphy case is now treated with reserve by some researchers. Many spiritualists felt that Bernstein, although sincere in his account of the sessions, had been misled and that under hypnosis Virginia Tighe acted as the unconscious medium for the deceased and somewhat mischievous spirit of Bridey Murphy who was delighted to take advantage of the opportunity of chatting to the world she had left some ninety years before.

In 'Lady Alice Browning' we have yet another apparent incarnation of Peggy Bailey and for the first time we encounter a crippling physical defect, some form of paralysis, possibly infantile or essential paralysis once prevalent in young children – a disease that can affect both legs but is not generally of uniform distribution. The affected muscles rapidly waste and become flaccid and cease to respond to electrical or any stimulation whatever. Heredity often plays a part in paralytic diseases and it would be interesting to discover the lineage of 'Alice Browning'; unfortunately research along these lines has so far proved unproductive.

I have been unable to trace 'Sir George Browning' in any volume of *Who's Who* or the *Dictionary of National Biography*. I have been equally unsuccessful in less obvious places of research and in all the circumstances I have to say that it seems likely to me either that no such person ever existed or that, if he did, he lived at a different period, at a different place and in different conditions.

With the 'appearance' of 'Alice Browning' the scene has shifted to 1903 and, it seems, we glimpse life at that time through the eyes of a paralysed girl; the daughter of 'Sir George Browning', a former colonel in the Indian Army and now a banking executive living in a large house overlooking St James's Park, possibly The Mall.

The location of her father's bank is given without hesitation as "The Strand", and one immediately thinks of the banking house of Coutts, established in 1692 as Middleton and Campbell in St Martin's Lane. Later it became Campbell and

Bruce and in 1754 James Coutts became a partner when the
name was changed to Campbell and Coutts. Thomas Coutts
became a partner in 1761 when Campbell died and when
James Coutts died in 1778 Thomas Coutts (1735–1822) took
full control and he became the richest man in London in his
time (so it is claimed).

Coutts and Company moved to 440 Strand in 1904, so if the
information given by 'Alice Browning' is correct her father
was at the bank (if it *was* Coutts's Bank where he was
employed) during the time the bank moved from 59 Strand
(where it had been since 1737) to 440 Strand. If this were so he
would doubtless have mentioned the fact, perhaps even talked
about the matter to some extent, which may have been the
reason that 'Alice' immediately responded with 'The Strand'
when asked the location of her father's bank. Coutts's Bank
remained in the Strand until 1973 when Head Office was
moved to 1 Suffolk Street, SW1.

Unfortunately my enquiries at Coutts and Company in an
endeavour to trace anyone who might fit the name or available
description of 'Sir George Browning' have been unproductive.

The stated location of Alice's house is interesting. From the
information given: i.e. "a big house"; "near St James's Park";
and "overlooking the park"; everything points to the house
being located in The Mall, but this is unlikely.

The buildings in The Mall are built on land that was
formerly part of St James's Park. Marlborough House, for
example, was built by Wren in 1709–10 for the Duke of
Marlborough on the site of the pheasantry of St James's Park
and George IV, when Regent, proposed to connect Carlton
House with Marlborough House and St James's Palace by a
gallery, but Nash's speculation in buying Carlton House and
Gardens and overlaying St James's Park with terraces was
approved and plans for a National Gallery that would have
been superior to Versailles were abandoned. All this makes it
unlikely that 'Sir George Browning' lived in The Mall. Where
then was the house?

There is too the tantalizing reference to "a carriage step
outside with a statue of a little black boy". Will this help us to
identify the elusive home of 'Sir George Browning'? No such
statue is listed by John Timbs among the sixty-six principal

outdoor statues, which is understandable, and I have been unable to find any reference to such a statue in any reference book on London. The only statue in The Mall listed in Godfrey Thompson's *London Statues* (1971) is that of George VI; although this book is only intended to include statues designed to represent historic personages. It occurred to me that the author, during research for the book, may have come across reference to such a statue, or know of a statue answering the description, but once again my enquiries yielded no information.

Alice said she had read de Vere Stacpoole's *The Blue Lagoon*, a book published in 1909 which was enormously popular and won fame for its author. Its theme, a boy and a girl alone on a desert island, was considered daring at the time it appeared, a fact that de Vere Stacpoole must have found amusing in his later years for he did not die until 1951; but Alice's description and immediate reaction ("I wasn't supposed to read it") are accurate and completely in character for the period.

So with *Alice in Wonderland*, a book published in 1865 and probably the most famous and popular children's story ever published. 'Alice Browning' (who may have been particularly attracted to the book because she had the same name as the central character) said the book was her favourite because "it's very amusing"; a somewhat surprising remark one might think for a young teenager who maintained that she was always reading it. Of course it *is* amusing but from a child's point of view it might be thought that she would find it fun, perhaps dream-like, entertaining, witty, fully of imagination, odd, extravagant, ridiculous, quaint, wonderful, even fascinating, but not, I would have thought, amusing. But then *Alice in Wonderland* has many facets and part of its success is due to its wide and varied appeal to many people.

During the relaxed conversation about this classic children's book, the hypnotist (who also knows and enjoys the book) has remarked on a slight suggestion of Peggy Bailey's real voice coming through for a moment. The fact that he mentions this inconsistency is a sound pointer to his honest approach and his ever-vigilant and open mind.

Lewis Carroll did in fact write a couple of children's books after *Alice* (1865) and *Through the Looking Glass* (1871) – *Sylvie and Bruno* in 1889 and *Sylvie and Bruno Concluded* (1893) – but they sought to embody Christian philosophy and were confused and unsuccessful. He is best remembered, apart from his Alice books, for his nonsense verse and it is perhaps a little surprising that 'Alice Browning' does not seem to be aware of Lewis Carroll's nonsense verse – which was indeed amusing.

'Alice Browning's' reference to "A glossy sort of thin paper coloured book, which tells all the things that are going on in Society" could conceivably have been *The Tatler* or possibly *Country Life*, both magazines carried colourwork and were much in vogue in 1912.

It will have been noticed that 'Alice Browning' was able to tell the hypnotist the correct name of the monarch at the time (1912): King George. He had come to the throne on 6 May 1910 and it is not unreasonable to accept that two years or so would seem 'some time' to a paralysed and lonely girl living out her life in a big house. She also correctly named the previous King, Edward.

The name of her favourite doctor is given as Sir Harold Somers (or Summers). It have been unable to trace any such doctor. There is no doubt that accurate names, dates and matters of fact are extremely difficult to obtain from apparently regressed subjects. It may be that such matters are long forgotten and have been replaced by far more important things and when recalled, if they can be recalled at all, they are vague and uncertain and distorted. Be this as it may, it makes life very difficult for the investigator seeking collaboration and substantiation of the character revealed. There is too the idea that what is obtained at these 'age-regression' sessions is in fact a psychic memory that 'dresses' itself in a few facts. To attempt to establish or relate such 'facts' with reality presents the unbiased investigator with momentous problems.

With 'Alice Browning' the hypnotist again obtained a touching and realistic death-bed scene and in rather more detail than in the case of Sally Fraser. Speaking partly in the past tense at this session suggests that although she may be reliving her past, she is conscious that it *is* the past and inevitably the spectre of role-taking rears its head again; for if the hypnotist has truly succeeded in bringing back a personality from a previous life at a given time, how can that person speak in the past tense about activities and actions that are alleged to be happening *at that precise time?* If, however, the personality communicating was an invention, conscious or unconscious, it is not unlikely that when reaching the death of that personality, the communicator would revert to the past tense in describing events at the time of her 'death', since she knew that this was merely an interlude in her existence. The use of the past tense at this time suggests either that the communicator is role-taking or that the essential 'soul' or 'spirit' had already left 'Alice' and treats her existence as a thing of the past.

The 'Alice Browning' episode ends dramatically with the girl, paralysed all her life, finding that she can walk! If this is role-taking, it is character impersonation of a very high order. One question that has to be answered is, would anyone attempting to concoct a personality think of healing a physical defect after death? It is a question more easily asked than answered.

So it is with much of the research into reincarnation that has been carried out in recent years, and some idea of this work, its implications and the informed opinions of those concerned with such work, is important in any attempt at a valuation of the present case or cases of apparent regression to previous lives.

Particularly interesting – even important – is the work of Professor Ian Stevenson who presented some of his extensive research in *Twenty Cases Suggestive of Reincarnation*, published by the American Society for Psychical Research in 1966.

During the course of investigating the claims of a five-year-old child who, over a period of three years, seemed to recall an earlier life in another town, including names and descriptions of people and places and detailed accounts of particular incidents, Dr Stevenson encountered many conflicting items and puzzling incidents.

Formerly head of the department of psychiatry at the University of Virginia, Dr Stevenson – after personal investigation – concluded that the boy's claim consisted of fifty-seven specific details regarding a former life; he also separated forty-seven older pertinent items reported by the boy's family and, especially interesting, he elicited ten new 'facts' from the boy himself. Of these 114 claims Dr Stevenson believed he established that a staggeringly high proportion, fifty-one details, were in fact correct.

Then came the surprise: the details applied not to any deceased person whom the boy had named and whom his parents believed had been a previous incarnation of their son, but to a man with the same name who was alive and well! And then it was discovered that, to a certain degree, the facts also applied to another man, with the same surname, who had died in the manner described by the boy; but there were problems in attributing most of the other details to the dead man, and when the dead man's son was questioned at length by Dr Stevenson it became apparent that many of the original claims could not be substantiated and not only that – they applied to a remarkable degree to a dead cousin who had lived nearby!

Dr Stevenson decided to take the boy to the town he claimed to have lived in during his previous incarnation and to see, in particular, whether he could identify the building he had (apparently) lived in and describe its interior. In actual fact the boy did not do particularly well in identification of the house or various parts of the town, but the places had changed considerably over the years.

Concerning the interior of the house (which had been closed for some years), the boy accurately listed sixteen correct statements of identification and there seemed to be grounds for accepting that there was some relationship between the 'memories' of the boy and the experiences of the deceased man; but was it evidence for reincarnation?

Dr Stevenson, who has studied the evidence of over six hundred people who claimed to have memories of previous lives, has reached no firm conclusions about reincarnation, but his work is fascinating and forcibly demonstrates the difficulties and problems – and surprises – in store for researchers in these mysterious realms.

9

The Tiverton Investigations

The weather in Devon was warm and sunny. Despite our keen interest it was with some effort that we secluded ourselves in the dark shade of the local reference libraries. The one at Tiverton, steeped in an aura of history, was quite fruitful in our search. We were soon lost to the present in the fading pages of old parish records.

It was obvious that the Frasers and Barnes, being plain country folk, would not have had any personal references. These were reserved for the ways of the rich and the deeds of the poor. However, a number of local events had been recorded during the period in which we were interested. I made particular note of these with the intention of testing out Sally's knowledge on our return to London. We did spend some considerable time exploring all the churchyards in the locality where Sally and Sam might have been laid to rest. No gravestones could be found that went back to the 1700s, although there were several from which the inscriptions had become completely obliterated with age.

Our West Country holiday over, we returned home and planned to have a session with the Baileys as soon as possible. Somehow, this did not prove at all easy. With the summer and fine weather with us, Bill's flying commitments were now considerable and he frequently flew seven days a week. Summer slowly passed and as the time since our last session with Peggy lengthened, so the days shortened. Joan and I were getting married at the end of the year. Plans had to be made and a home arranged. My notes on Tiverton lay quietly, securely and frustratingly in a drawer in my consulting room.

Six months passed. At last, one long winter's evening in February 1969, we did eventually meet for our Tiverton check-up. The transcript from the recording made at the time speaks for itself:

". . . Today, Peggy, you are six. This is your sixth birthday. How old are you?"

"I'm six." (The voice of a six-year-old.)

"How old, dear?"

"Six."

"And what are you going to do today, Peggy?"

"It's my birthday."

"You're having a party, are you, dear?"

"No." (Pensively.)

"Aren't you? Oh, why not?"

"My mummy's busy."

"Is she? What is she busy doing?"

"Looking after me and looking after John."

"Who is John?"

"He's my little brother."

"Is he?"

"Yes."

"Oh, I see. Right. And what is your second name, Peggy?"

"Frances . . ."

"Peggy Frances what?"

"No, it's not Peggy really."

"What is it?"

"It's Margaret." (With the honest accuracy of a child.)

"But they call you Peggy, do they?"

"Yes."

"I see. All right, dear. I want you to go back in time and you're getting younger and younger. [She took a deep breath.] You're going back in time to your second birthday. Today, little girl, you are two. How old are you? [She hesitated.] Today you are two. Two years old today. Now tell me, how old are you?"

"Two." (She almost cooed the word.)

"How old, dear?"

"Two." (The exact voice of a two-year-old.)

"And what is your name, little girl?"

"Peg-gy."

"Peggy what?"

"Peggy." (Almost as though she did not appreciate that

there could be more than just one name.)

"Peggy."

"Yes."

"And do you know where you live?"

"In a flat." (Slightly unsure.)

"I see. And who do you live with?"

"My mummy . . ."

"Yes."

"And my daddy."

"Yes."

"Mummy and daddy (reconsidering) . . . and little baby."

"And what is little baby's name?"

". . . little boy."

"Little boy?"

"Yes."

"What's his name, dear?"

"John-John." (She pronounced it like a double-barrelled name.)

"John-John?"

"John-John, yes."

"Right. You're going back in time. You're going back in time, back, back, back. You're going back now in time [she took a very deep breath as though in anticipation of what was to come], a long time, to the time when you were someone else living on this earth. Back in time to when you were someone else living on this earth. I'm going to give you a date and I want you to go back to that time. [I was not prepared for her to choose either the 'life' or date at this session, the idea, of course, being to check up on the information I had brought back from Tiverton.] I want you to go back now [she took yet another deep breath], to go back now a little over two hundred years to the year 1756. Going back, going back to the year 1756, when you were someone living on this earth. 1756. [A very deep breath.] And now, tell me who you are and what is your name? [A pause, while she breathed a little deeply.] That's right. You've told me before and you will tell me now. The year 1756." (Another deep breath, as though she were fighting her way through the mists of the past and slowly orientating herself. This was the first time I had deliberately chosen 1756. On previous occasions with Sally, she had either presented me with the date or I had started her off as the young girl of seventeen, around 1733.]

"Sally Barnes." (The immediate Devon burr.)

"Hello, Sally. Haven't met you for some time now, have I?"

"No. (With great respect.) It's a long time."

"How are you keeping?"

"Oh, I'm very fit, thank you."

"It's 1756. Now, how old are you now, about?"

"Oh, I'm nearly forty." (Without any hesitation. This age is quite correct. She was born in 1716.)

"That's quite right. That's quite right. [I was impressed by her immediate accuracy.] You're forty this year, aren't you?"

"Yes."

"Yes."

"Yes. And tell me, how's your husband?"

"Oh, he's very well."

"What's his name? I've forgotten now."

"Oh, my Sam. You know my Sam." (Playfully scolding me.)

"Of course, I know your Sam. And how about your children, how are they?"

"Oh, they're busy, you know. Here and there."

"How many have you got?"

"Why, just the two."

"And what are their names?"

"Mary."

"Yes."

"And Terry."

"And where do they live?"

"Oh, they live with us still."

"They do?"

"Yes." (The tone of her reply seemed to suggest surprise that I should have asked such an obvious question. The Sally personality was now well and truly established.)

"Are they married?"

"No. Terry's getting married soon."

"Who's Terry marrying?"

"Joan." (But she sounded a little unsure.)

"Joan, is it?"

"Yes." (Hesitatingly.)

"Are you sure?"

"Yes." (Unconvincingly. In the earlier recording she had called the girl Janie. In her Devon drawl Joan and Jane were similar. Nevertheless, this slight discrepancy seemed to be concerning her. She obviously felt that something was wrong in her answer. I found her honesty in this respect quite fascinating. What also impressed me was her accuracy with ages. In the first recording she had told me, when she was forty-five, that Terry had married Janie. This time, when she is forty, Terry is going to get married.)

"Mm. Right. Do you ever go round to any of the other villages near where you live, Sally?"

"Well, we go through them."

"What is the name of your village, where you live?"

"Where I live?"

"Mm."

"Oh, we're on a farm."

"Yes, but where is it? Do you know? If I were to say . . . if someone were to ask me how I get to your farm, how would I tell them?"

"Oh, they go to Whimple."

"They go to where?"

"Whimple."

"And . . . how do you spell that, please?"

"Oh, I'm not very good at spelling things."

"Could you just pronounce it for me once more?"

"Wim-poll." (Deliberately)

"Wim-poll?"

"Yes."

"And where is it exactly? Is it near another place? Can you give me the name of another place that it's near?"

"Well, just the nearest place is Whimple."

"I see. I see. [There is a Whimple to the east of the Exe and about seven miles from where I believe Sally claims to have lived. It may, of course, be much nearer.] And do you ever go into Tiverton very much?"

"I have been, but I don't go out very much, really."

"But I suppose you get news about what's happening in Tiverton and Exeter, do you?"

"Well, Sam tells me sometimes."

"I see. I see. Now this is the year, as I said, 1756, and I

understand that there have been certain occurrences in Tiverton [She took a deep breath quite spontaneously. This was interesting as I was not at this point either regressing or progressing her. She may have been preparing herself to remember the occurrences to which I was referring. In which case this was a quick anticipation.] that you are bound to know about. Er, about fifteen years ago, when you were about twenty-five, something happened in Tiverton, something that killed a lot of people. [Another deep breath.] Can you tell me about it?"

"Killed people?"

"Well, a lot of people died in Tiverton about fifteen years ago approximately, Sally."

"Well, there was the plague."

"Yes. [Although the great outbreak, the Black Death, occurred in England in 1348 and the plague of London took place in 1665, isolated epidemics were certainly possible in Sally's time.] Do you know how many people died from the plague?"

"In Tiverton, you mean?"

"Yes."

"Oh, I think lots and lots of people there."

"You don't know how many exactly, do you?"

"Oh no."

"What sort of plague?"

"They said a bu-, a bu-, a bubonic plague or somethin'." (She pronounced it *boobonic*.)

"Really, what, in 1741?" (Bubonic plague was transmitted by fleas from infected rats which had died.)

"Some word like that, yes."

"And what did they do with the people that died?"

"Oh, they put'm in a big hole."

"Were none of them buried in the churchyard at all?"

"They may have been."

"But you don't know?"

"I think they was in a big hole."

"I see. Can you go back in your mind? Can you remember what happened? Something happened in Tiverton when you were about . . . when you were a little girl [A short, deep breath.] of about fifteen. Can you remember what happened to Tiverton? Something very serious happened to the town."

"Tiverton?" (Slightly alarmed.)

"Yes. In fact it was during 1731, when you were fifteen. [Yet another deep breath.] It was such a serious thing that you must have known. Something very serious happened to the town when you were fifteen."

"Fifteen." (Pensively.)

"When you were a little girl."

"Fifteen." (In a whisper to herself as she considered.)

"Sally, go back in time. Go back in time to when you were eighteen years of age. Sally, go back in time [deep breath] to when you were eighteen. You are now eighteen years old, Sally. How old are you, Sally? [Several rather deep breaths.] Back in time. You are now eighteen. You are now eighteen and the year is approximately 1734. How old are you, Sally?"

"I'm eighteen."

"What is your name, dear?"

"Sally Fraser." (A delightful roll to the 'r'.)

"Aha. And where do you live?"

"I live on a farm."

"And where is the farm? Where is it near?"

"Well, it's in a lot of fields and the river runs by."

"Now Sally, if you walk from your farm down to the river [A deep breath. I do not know why.], which way would you have to turn to go to Tiverton? Would you turn left or right?"

"I would turn right."

"You would turn right?"

"Yes."

"I see. I see. Thank you. Have you ever heard of Bickleigh?"

"Yes, a little village."

"Mm. Anything else about Bickleigh?"

"I don't know."

"Would you have to go through Bickleigh if you went to Tiverton? Do you know?"

"Yes."

"Hm, thank you. Sally, a few years ago, two, three or four years ago, something rather serious happened in Tiverton, to the town of Tiverton. Can you tell me what it was, dear? [Deep breath.] You must have heard because a great disaster happened to Tiverton. Just a few years ago. Can you tell me what it was? [She hestitated.] It doesn't matter if you can't remember but I'm interested, you see."

"What's a 'disaster'?" (I found her not knowing the meaning of the word 'disaster' quite exciting. The process of hypnotism had so completely transformed Peggy Bailey into Sally Fraser that even that everyday word was now meaningless to this poorly educated country girl in 1734.)

"Well, something happened to the town. The town was damaged."

"Oh, somethin' bad?"

"Mm. You may not have heard, of course, but I think you might have done."

"How long did you say?" (She actually asked me to repeat the question. I interpreted this as a sign of active interest.)

"About three or four years ago, approximately, when you were about fifteen, something like that."

"Oh, fire!"

"Yes, it was a fire! That's quite true."

"Yes."

"Quite true."

"Lots of things burnt."

"I don't suppose you know what part of the town the fire started in, what street, do you?"

"Oh no, but it was somethin' with a baker to do." (Trying hard to remember.)

"It might have been. I don't know. Have you heard of Gold Street?"

"No."

"You haven't?"

"Not that I know of."

"There was a fire in Tiverton. That's quite right, dear. That's quite right."

"Yes, I didn't hear very much."

"You didn't?"

"No."

"I want you to come forward in time to the year 1740 (a deep breath) and you are now about twenty-four. Sally, you are now about twenty-four and the year is about 1740. What is your name, dear?"

"I'm Sally Barnes."

"Tell me, Sally. I'm interested in the history (deep breath) of Tiverton and if you happen to know I'd like you to tell me, but it doesn't matter if you don't remember. Something happened in Tiverton. There was quite a lot of news and a lot of noise in Tiverton about two or three years ago. There was a Mr Grimes who lived at the Red Lion Inn in Pound Hill (deep breath) and he was involved in an incident. Can you tell me what it was? There was a man whose name was Mr Grimes. There was a man who lived at the Inn, the Red Lion on Pound Hill. You know Pound Hill, do you?"

"I'm not sure."

"You're not sure?"

"I jes' know it is a place."

"Yes, well what was the incident? I don't know. I was wondering if you might be able to help me."

"Mr Grimes." (To herself.)

"Well, there was an incident about this man who lived at the Red Lion Inn."

"I'll think now. I'll think. How long ago?" (She was trying to be helpful.)

"Oh, about two or three years, something like that."

"Oh, two or three years. (She considered.) Oh, someone got murdered, didn't they, there? There was somebody got murdered there, sometime."

"Well, there's something in what you say."

"They said 'e was murdered, anyway. Oh, there was a robbery, lots of trouble. It's not a very nice place. I don't go there."

"All right, thank you, dear. Thank you, dear. I want you to come forward in time. I want you to come forward in time (deep breath) to when you were forty again, to when you were forty again. To 1756. To 1756. How old are you now, Sally?"

"I'm forty now." (Voice more mature.)

"Mm. About three years ago, Sally, (deep breath) one of the rivers overflowed and did a lot of damage. I'm sure you know all about it. One of the rivers near Tiverton, near the Exe, overflowed and did a lot of damage. Do you remember that?"

"The Axe has overflowed." (About fifteen miles to the east.)

"Mm."

"Yes."

"There was another river round there that overflowed, wasn't there, near the Exe?"

"Well, they'm all overflowing, 'cos the rain."

"Well, can you tell me the name of any other river near the Exe."

"The Axe, the Axe, not the Exe. The Axe." (Correcting me.)

"Yes. Can you tell me the name of any other river near where you live other than the Exe and Axe? Do you know, dear?"

"Yes. I think some more rivers."

"Can you just tell me the name of one or two, please. I'd be very grateful to you."

"The Dart. There's the Dart."

"Mm. Is that near you?"

"Oh, it's a little way. It's a good way but there's the Dart." (My estimation is that she lived approximately eighteen miles from the Dart. However, the Little Dart was only about eight miles away.)

"Aha."

"That overflowed, too."

"Yes. What else, dear?"

"Er . . . near us? How near do you want to know?"

"Within three or four miles, something like that. Well, say within five or ten miles. We'll make it easier for you, shall we?"

"Oh, ah, well let me see . . ."

"Have you heard of the River Culm?"

"Yes. [Uncertainly.] I don't know it very well."

"Do you know the River Lowman?"

"No."

"You don't know it?"

"No."

"I see. Tell me, I'm going to give you the name of a few places and see if you know the name of them. [Deep breath.] Do you know . . . have you heard of Bantin's Farm?"

"Bantin's? Yes." (Not really sure.)

"Is it near you?"

"It's a few miles."

"Mm. Is it on your side of the river or would you have to cross the river to get to it?"

"No. It's on our side."

"Actually, I don't think it is on your side. Never mind, dear. Have you heard of Land's Foot?"

"No."

"Or Hollwell?"

"No."

"Have you heard of Ashley?"

"Yes."

"Have you heard of Mogridge?"

"No." (During these last questions she had sounded genuinely concerned that she knew hardly any of the places I had mentioned. Not so much, I sensed, for her own sake but rather that she was being unhelpful.)

"These are places all very near you, Sally, you know. All very near you."

"But I don't know many . . . " (She was a little distressed.)

"Don't you know them? Never mind, dear?"

"I don't go very far, you see. We'm busy with the farm. It's a big farm."

"Have you heard of . . . Does the word Blundell mean anything to you? Blundell. It's a very well-known name in your part of the world. Blundell."

"He'm a big house."

"Yes. It is a big house."

"A big kind of a . . . well, a squire there."

"A squire?"

"Yes."

"What else, what else? This is 1756, we said, didn't we? Yes. What else can you tell me about this house? Is it used for something, do you think? [She thought for a moment.] Well, shall I tell you?"

"No. I'm thinking what you might mean by that."

"Well, this big house is used for something. It's known as Blundell's something. Do you know?"

"It's Blundell's Reach, they call it."

"Mm. I see. Well, actually, there's a place in Tiverton called Blundell's school. It's an old school."

"No . . ."

"You don't know it? Never mind, dear."

"No! . . . Jest a big house!"

"Mm. Have you heard of Samuel Wesley?"

"No."

"Well, you've heard of John Wesley?"

"Yes." (Not really convinced.)

"Tell me about John Wesley. [She pondered for a few moments. How could I expect her to know that when she did not even know the meaning of the word 'disaster'. Yet I had to try.] Never mind, dear. It doesn't matter. Never mind, dear. It doesn't matter. I want you to go forward in time. I want you to go forward in time a little, forward in time, forward in time to when you were sixty. I want you to go forward in time, Sally, to when you were sixty. [A deep breath.] How old are you, Sally?"

"Oim sixty, now." (A much older voice.)

"Are you? And how are you, keeping well?"

"Oh, fairly well, I think. Yes, Not too bad."

"Tell me, how's Beauty?" (The dog she had mentioned months before when the recording machine did not work.)

"My Beauty. She'm gettin' old, poor old thing. She's still waggin' her tail."

"How old is she, now?"

"Oh, I 'spect she'll be about twelve or something like that. She'm getting old."

"Is she?"

"Yes."

"And how about the men on the farm?"

"Oh, you mean Job? (Also mentioned before at the same session as Beauty.)

"Yes, I mean Job."

"Ah."

"How's he?"

"Aha! [Almost with a chuckle.] He's a rare one, he is. A rare one, he is."

"And there's another man. What was his name?"

"Job . . . Job? . . ." (Thinking.)

"Mm. I know Job's your favourite. But isn't there another man who helps sometimes?"

"Yes, they'm another one. Yes, oh dear, I jus' don' even remember names now."

"Pardon."

"Can't remember names now." (Slightly concerned.)

"Well, it was Harry, wasn't it?"

"Well, oh no, it's not Harry. No."

"Isn't it? You told me once it was Harry."

"No." (In a drawl.)

"Isn't it? But I know you like Job, don't you?"

"Yeh, he'm nice. He'm nice, is Job, yes."

"How's Sam?"

"Oh, my poor old Sam is gone."

"Is he? A long time?"

(A sigh.) "No, no, not very long, no."

"Sally, I want you to go back in time again. Go back in time to when you were thirty. [Deep breath.] Going back about thirty years. Today, Sally, you are thirty. Today is your thirtieth birthday. How old are you today, Sally?"

"Oh, I'm thirty today." (A vigorous, healthy voice.)

"And how's Sam?"

"Oh, he's just fine."

"And the children?"

"Yes. They'm growing up now."

"Are you going to do anything special today?"

"Well, they're going to do some of my work for me, so's I don't have to be so busy today."

"How nice for you."

"Yes."

"Sally, I'm interested in your part of the country and I've been to one or two places but I'm not quite sure of the names, dear. [She took a deep breath without apparent reason, perhaps in anticipation of answering some questions.] If I ask you the names of places, I'd be interested to know if you've heard of them. Do you mind?"

"Oh no, I don't mind." (Helpfully.)

"Tell me, have you heard of a place called Burn?"

"Burn? Yes."

"You have?"

"Burn, yes."

"Any idea of where it may be? Would it be to the west or to the east do you think, or don't you know?"

"Well, let me think now. Burn? Oh, east, west, oh!"

"If you're not sure, don't guess."

"No."

"You're not sure. All right. Have you heard of Stoke Canon?"

"Yes, that's a place."

"Hm, hm. Have you heard of Bramford Speke?"

"Yes."

"Have you heard of Bickleigh Castle?"

"Yes."

"Where is it, dear?"

"How do you mean?"

"Where is Bickleigh Castle? How would I get to it from your farm?"

"Oh, you would go towards Exeter to get to Bickleigh."

"I see. You're quite sure, are you?"

"Yes."

"So if you went to the river from your house, would you turn left or right to get to Bickleigh?"

"I would turn from my house right."

"You would?"

"To Bickleigh? Yes."

"Have you heard of Upton Pine or Upton Pinn?" (Two possible ways of pronouncing Upton Pyne.)

"No."

"Have you heard of a place called Cowley?"

"Yes."

"And how about a place called Luppitt?" (This is about eighteen miles to the east.)

"No."

"Are you sure?"

"No."

"All right. Have you heard of Silverton?"

"No."

"Is there a castle at Exeter?" (The castle is, in fact, Rougemont Castle.)

"A castle at. . .? There's Bitby."

"There is?"

"There's Bitby Castle, yes."

"There is? Right, thank you very much. Thank you very much. Right Sally, you're going forward in time, [I felt she had had enough.] forward in time, forward in time about two hundred years. Forward in time, forward in time, back to the

present time, back to the present time [a deep breath] and you
are now once again Peggy Bailey. You are now back to the
present time and you are lying on the couch in Leonard's
consulting room [another deep breath as she returned through
time] enjoying a nice, lovely, hypnotic sleep. Today is
Monday, 16th February, 1959 and you're lying in a deep
hypnotic sleep and you feel comfortable and happy. What is
your name?"

"Peggy." (Her own familiar voice.)

"Peggy what?"

"Bailey."

"And do you feel well, Peggy?"

"Yes, thank you."

"Enjoying the hypnosis, are you?"

"Oh yes."

"Good show."

Should I have felt disappointed that Sally was able to identify
so few places in her local environment or unable to make
positive comment on major events? I suppose I did. But yet,
was it all that surprising? Sally's life would have been confined
almost exclusively to the small world of her farm. Although
pleasant and friendly, she had not enjoyed the opportunity of
an education and, as mentioned before, she did not even
understand the meaning of the word 'disaster'. She was hardly
worldly in the modern sense.

Peggy Bailey was the only deep trance subject I had
investigated so far. I had to decide in those early days whether
to carry out further exhaustive tests on her or find out if other
subjects would produce similar results for me. I decided on the
latter course, which decision at that time, I am sure, was the
correct one. Perhaps it was that choice then which resulted in
the long time lapse which is now making the present
investigations of Peggy so interesting.

During the following three or four years I regressed several
good deep trance subjects and compiled an interesting library
of recordings. I have had a young lady who claimed to have
come from the court of Louis XIV and recounted her life to me
in French. I have sat enthralled while a young Manchester
business-man (who was born between the two world wars)

was shot down at the controls of his First World War German fighter plane after a dog-fight with a British Sopwith Camel, all, of course, in German. I have listened to a local housewife tell the sad tale of her mother in old London, thrown into a pond and drowned for being a witch. The subjects I used had all been known to me for some time. I had established in each case that he or she was a good deep trance subject, capable of being regressed in this life-time before attempting a regression back to 'a previous life'. In all cases the subjects had agreed to experimentation but had accepted beforehand that I would not disclose the precise nature.

Yet all the time my strongest sentiments stayed with Sally, Liza and Alice. Perhaps, because Sally was my very first 'discovery', my greatest attachment was to her. A number of years had passed since I last 'met' her. In that time I had accumulated so much additional material that to have acquired more would, indeed, have overloaded my collection of tape-recordings.

During these years my professional commitments had increased. I had become involved in post-graduate activities and I found that I was having very little time for other interests. Even my time for flying was encroached upon. With my great love of the sport, this was a painful sacrifice. I saw little of the Baileys. The opportunity for further hypnosis with Peggy became less and less. At the back of my mind I knew that one day I would have to investigate Peggy Bailey again. It occurred to me that if I waited a very long time how interesting it would be to see if she would produce the same results again. I discussed the idea with Peter Underwood, whose eager acceptance to participate fired me with my old enthusiasm.

Seventeen years had elapsed since I had first heard the words, "Sally Fraser … sir." The time had come to turn back the clock to those early days of the eighteenth century. I approached Bill and Peggy Bailey. As I had expected, they were most willing to co-operate. Once again, I gave Bill a detailed plan of my intentions. Peggy was quite happy to know that I wished to recontinue the hypnosis started many years previously.

So now, in 1974, the scene is set for the reinvestigations.

The cast is to be the same: Peggy Bailey, the subject; myself as hypnotist; my wife, Joan, and Bill Bailey as witnesses; but this time with one very important addition, Peter Underwood as psychic investigator, critic and evaluator.

The couch in my consulting room is older, well worn and perhaps just a little lumpy in places. It patiently waits to bear the gentle weight of Peggy Bailey again.

10
Assessment and Discussion IV

The apparent regression of Peggy Bailey to 'Sally Fraser' after the Wilders' visit to Devon, armed with information obtained at previous sessions, is important and well repays close study. The first question that arises is, how can one guard against hypnotic suggestibility?

It has to be admitted that when Leonard Wilder hypnotized Peggy Bailey in February 1959 all his conscious mind was concentrated on the character, characteristics and environment of 'Sally Fraser'. Leonard and his wife had spent some time at Tiverton and elsewhere seeking evidence for the existence of Sally and her family, the location of the farm, and any other facts that might help to establish the reality of the person who claimed to be a previous incarnation of Peggy Bailey. What effect would this have on the susceptible, receptive and open mind of Peggy Bailey as she lay, relaxed and subservient to the proficient will of the hypnotist? After all, one definition of hypnosis is that it is a condition of heightened suggestibility. Yet hypnosis is also the peculiar condition which enables certain phenomena to occur although it is not the means of exciting them; and suggestibility is inherent in all human beings.

Yet, *if* Leonard Wilder unconsciously (or for that matter consciously) influenced the mind of Peggy Bailey while she was under hypnosis, surely she would have related information that was known to the hypnotist instead of continually getting nowhere when questions were asked concerning places and events apparently pertinent to Sally Fraser and her world; what should have been forthcoming should have been fact after fact that corresponded with the Wilders' information. Since this did not happen we have to look elsewhere for any rational explanation.

It seems likely that in many, perhaps most, of the cases of apparent regression, little explanation is necessary other than the dramatization of material which has at some time been known to the subject but is not consciously remembered, and it may be that under hypnosis these forgotten memories surface and in the face of unconscious suggestion from the hypnotist, or someone else, take on the form of other lives. It is possible of course for facts to be 'photographically' imprinted on the mind although the subject is unaware that this has happened and is absolutely sincere in insisting that he knows nothing of the matters in question.

There are many instances of such happenings. One concerned a doctor in Canada who found that a hypnotized patient was talking in an obscure language not used for over two thousand years. When no one could be found who understood the spoken language, the subject was asked to write down what he had to say. The words he laboriously wrote were discovered to be a series of magical Oscan curses which used to be inscribed on rolls and thrown into graves for the purpose of gaining control over infernal entities.

'Oscan' was the Romans' name for a dialect spoken by the Osci of Campania, probably introduced by the invading Samnites in the fifth century BC. The dialect was also used in the extreme south of Italy and part of Sicily some three hundred years BC. Oscan was gradually replaced by Latin. I have seen Oscan inscriptions scratched on the walls of houses at Pompeii shortly before the eruption of Vesuvius in AD 79. Traces of the Oscan dialect survive today in modern Southern Italy.

The patient, out of hypnosis, had not studied Latin and had never heard of Oscan; he was completely ignorant of what he had written but it was identified as authentic Oscan. Was this evidence of a previous existence on the part of the patient? It began to look like it until it was discovered that some time previously the subject had been in a library looking up references in preparation for an examination that he was to sit, when his thoughts began to wander and he day-dreamed. A book lay open on the table before him at a page headed 'The Curse of Vibia' and below the ancient curse was printed in

Oscan. It seems likely that the words impressed themselves photographically and quite unconsciously on his mind and he would have sworn that he knew nothing about the matter and had never heard of the Oscan language and this would have been right, as far as his conscious mind was concerned.

Is it possible that 'Sally Fraser' and 'Liza' and 'Alice Browning' are fantasies clothed in forgotten facts that lie hidden in Peggy Bailey's subconscious? Certainly she is interested in history and reads historical novels and it must be said that as far as could be established, so far, no facts had been produced that *could* not have been acquired by Peggy Bailey in her normal waking life; and perhaps the convincing authenticity of the various periods lends support to this theory for once 'inside' a period everything the subject had ever heard or read about that period would contribute to producing realism, accuracy and exactness of a precision undreamed of in normal circumstances. Yet this did not happen. There were mistakes and unexpected gaps in what should have been total recall of a bygone age.

It is often the case that subjects who are easily hypnotized are also very suggestible and it is interesting to recall the case known in the annals of psychical research as the 'Woman in Brown Case'. This concerned an alleged apparition that was seen thirteen times between November 1948 and May 1949 by a London office worker named in the report (preserved in the records of the Society for Psychical Research) as Miss Benson.

It is obvious that Miss Benson's imagination was fed by stories she heard of footsteps and figures being heard and seen in the office building which had been badly bombed in 1944 and practically rebuilt four years later; and before long she was telling everyone that she had seen an inexplicable 'woman in brown' several times.

The late Edward Osborn, an S.P.R. investigator and one-time editor of that Society's *Journal*, told me that following reports that another member of the staff, a Miss Dixon, had "walked into someone" who looked like a tall woman in brown, he stood at the spot indicated by Miss Dixon at approximately the same time that she had seen the figure and noticed that the street lamps outside caused a shadow to be cast on to a cupboard door, a shadow that grew darker as he approached, and he felt sure that this was the explanation for Miss Dixon's experience.

Turning to Miss Benson, he felt that the explanation for her repeatedly seeing a 'woman in brown' might possibly have some connection with what was in her mind just before she saw the figure. He discovered that Miss Benson was very suggestible and easily hypnotized. With her consent he hypnotized her and sought to discover what had been in her mind just before she saw the 'woman in brown' on each occasion. He discovered that her experience was preceded by her mind being occupied by an emotional complex from which she was suffering.

This, as so often is the case with a deep-seated complex, concerned guilt and death. Miss Benson related, in her normal state, that during the war she had been the first person to reach an A.R.P. post that had been bombed and there she was met by a man with badly cut arms while inside she found a woman lying in a pool of blood. She decided to do what she could for the man and afterwards felt guilty because she had not tried to save the woman.

Subsequent investigation showed that the story itself was a fantasy. Such an incident had in fact taken place but Miss Benson had not been present; she had only heard about it and it seems likely that the reason she imagined she had been involved and felt guilty about the part she thought she had played was what psychologists call a 'screen memory', which is a false picture unconsciously fabricated to blot out a real memory involving guilt. In these cases the guilt associated with the fantasy is easier to bear than the true memory that is blocked by the screen memory.

A possible memory that Miss Benson's fantasy was concealing concerned her mother's death. She was devoted to her mother and received a considerable shock when she was seventeen and arrived home one day to find her mother dead on the floor. So great was the shock that at first Miss Benson would not or could not accept the death of her mother and ever afterwards she was never able to talk about it. Psychologists consider that undue grief following the death of a loved one, coupled with feelings of guilt, is usually a sign that unconsciously there was some degree of hate as well as love in the relationship and that the subject is blaming herself, or himself, for their hidden feelings which they feel contributed to the death of their loved one.

While nothing of a similar nature is attributable to Peggy Bailey and the case under discussion, is it impossible that a somewhat similar *mechanism* could produce the convincing but, in the main, unsubstantiated lives of 'Sally Fraser', 'Liza Bloggs' and 'Alice Browning'? It is interesting to speculate on the possibility of three screen memories creating false pictures to obliterate unwelcome facts such as all of us experience during a lifetime, and certainly Peggy Bailey is open to psychological suggestion and is an excellent hypnotic subject. Everyone has memories that they prefer not to remember and it may be that in certain people an automatic trigger starts off a fantasy when something – be it a name, a date, a period, a feeling – begins a process of thought that could lead to repression of an unwelcome memory. Even under hypnosis this trigger action may work; possibly *especially* under hypnosis. Further research is indicated in these difficult, puzzling and frequently unrewarding reaches of the mind – that formidable and mysterious faculty with powers that defy description.

Medical men know that bodily changes are possible in response to mental attitudes, and a well-known example is the youth with 'crocodile skin' (a black horny layer that covered his whole body) who was cured, area by area, by hypnotic suggestion. The condition is generally incurable. On the basis of this and many other cases it has been suggested that it is likely that thought can affect direct changes in the body; after all, thought controls nervous impulses from the brain (if we accept that we have free will), and if thought can influence the movement of dice, as extensive experiments here and in America suggest it can, then it does appear likely that thought can indeed affect direct changes in the body. If we accept that, can we deny the possibility that thought – conditioned, distorted or misshapen by memory – may be able to produce lucid and plausible fantasy lives without the conscious knowledge of the person involved? In an effort to clothe the fantasy with every appearance of reality the material produced would include considerable 'atmosphere', sense of period and some facts, but the fundamental core of the story would have no foundation and any probing or questioning as to precise dates, places, people and facts that could be checked would be met with reluctance and eventual silence as the subconscious, willing to produce a coherent story, is unwilling to compound the deviation from the truth with downright inaccuracies that could be discovered.

Some idea of the enormous difficulties facing investigators in these regions can be obtained when it is appreciated that, taking the present case as an example, even if it were possible to establish that someone named Sally Fraser did live on a farm in Devon at the period stated and that every item had a foundation in fact, it would be necessary to show that Peggy Bailey could not have acquired this knowledge through normal − or paranormal − means; and the only conclusive proof that Peggy Bailey is *not* a reincarnation of Sally Fraser, or Liza Bloggs or Alice Browning, would necessitate an explanation of every scrap of relevant information that her 'regressed' personalities had produced.

Let us look at some of the information obtained from 'Sally Fraser' on this occasion. She consistently refers to her age dating from 1716 and immediately gives her age from that date when she apparently communicates in 1756, the year selected by the hypnotist. She names her two children, as she has done previously, Mary and Terry. Over two hundred years ago the life of a farmer's wife, such as Sally describes herself, would have been arduous, repetitive, isolated and unrewarding. Such people lived very close to nature, each family a tiny unit almost self-sufficient and hardly dependent at all on outsiders, apart from the sale of the produce from the farm. This would be organized at the weekly markets held in most towns of any size, but often the livestock, the eggs, butter and milk would be sold regularly by mutual agreement within the area of a few miles. These families were largely uneducated and their children were brought up to help on the farm from a very early age and they accepted without question the fact that they expected little more of life than to live on the same farm all their days, or perhaps marry and have a farm of their own. Sally lived in an exciting period when modern England was being born; but she would have known little about that. In 1740 there would have been about eight hundred market towns in England and Wales. Daniel Defoe (who died in 1731) has left behind – apart from his masterpiece *Robinson Crusoe* – a colourful and fascinating account of his travels throughout England, his admirable *Tour through the whole Island of Great Britain* (1724–26), and when he reached Devon he was delighted to find the domestic system of industry so strong. He writes: "Devonshire is full of great towns and these towns so full of people and those people so universally employed in trade and manufacture, that not only it cannot be equalled in England, but perhaps not in Europe."

The "great towns" he speaks of were small by today's standards and included Crediton, Tiverton and Honiton, none of them industrial towns any longer. But then in 1700 Devon was the third most populous county in the country, exceeded only by Worcestershire and Somerset!

The overall picture Sally paints of life on a Devon farm in the eighteenth century is an accurate one, with simplicity the key-word. But probing for topographical facts, no matter how gentle, meets with little success. True, it is stated that Sally's farm is near the village of Whimple, a village nine miles from Honiton to the east, nine from Exeter in the west and some seventeen miles from Tiverton (long noted for its lace) away to the north, beyond Beare and Bickleigh. The nearest village to Whimple is Talaton (present population 320) only a couple of miles away as the crow flies and it might be thought that Sally Fraser must have known Talaton.

Whimple has a somewhat surprisingly high population of 900 souls and there was an increase of about a hundred people in the fifteen years between 1946 and 1961. The reason may be that the famous Devon cyder orchards lie in this area and there is a cider factory within the parish. While Sally would not, of course, have known about cider factories, it might have been expected that at an opportune time she would have mentioned the growing of apples for cider. Although in her day cider-making would have been confined to the farms where the fruit was grown, cider played an important part in the life of the English countryman.

During the course of several conversations with 'Sally Fraser' a few references seemed worth following up and I therefore wrote to the Reverend H.T. Robins, thinking he was still rector of the parish of Whimple, but replying from Exeter, Mr Robins told me he had left Whimple after seventeen years.

I had asked Henry Robins whether he knew of any book or leaflet describing the village and St Mary's Church; or whether he had ever come across the name Fraser in the vicinity of Whimple. During the course of his most helpful reply (dated 11 May 1974) the Rev. Henry Robins told me that there was no available book or leaflet describing the village and church; there had been a leaflet (which was not entirely accurate) but it was no longer readily available, although the present rector of Whimple would probably have a copy. I made a note to write to the Rev. H.G. Tucker. Mr Robins went on to say that he had never heard of 'Fraser's Farm', nor could he remember the name Fraser occurring in any register; nor could he recollect a church dedicated to St Barnabas situated nearby. In view of all this uncertainty he was good enough to suggest that I might be confusing Whimple with Whipton, now within the City of Exeter boundary but once a separate parish. I do not think there is any question of the village being anything other than Whimple since, thanks to the care and foresight of Leonard Wilder, 'Sally' repeated the name twice and carefully pronounced it as "Wim-poll".

Mr Robins went on to say that Whimple is mentioned in Domesday Book when Buldwin the Sherriff held it and later it was held by Courtenary, Earl of Devon. The church, dedicated to St Mary the Virgin, was pulled down in 1843, except for the tower, and rebuilt with the addition of a south aisle in 1846.

In July, 1974, the Rev. H.G. Tucker loaned me a booklet of *Historical Notes of Whimple Parish Church*. Unfortunately it contained no relevant information. Mr Tucker searched the Index of the Parish Register from 1653 to 1836 but could find no reference to anyone named Fraser; and the other 'information' obtained from 'Sally Fraser' meant nothing to him.

Sally talks of people dying from "the plague", but of course there was no epidemic of plague – bubonic or any other infectious fever – in London or any part of England after 1666 although there were sporadic cases (which appear in bills of mortality) up to 1679. Although the disappearance of the plague has been attributed to the Great Fire of London and to quarantine, there were no great fires in other cities troubled by the plague and no effective quarantine was established until 1720, so while we do not know the reason for the cessation of the plague in England (which most authorities regard as spontaneous), we do know that there was no spectacular outbreak of plague at Tiverton or anywhere else in England during Sally's lifetime.

However her directions are generally accurate for getting to Tiverton from the vicinity of Whimple: she *would* turn right at the River Exe to get to Tiverton and she *would* pass through the village of Bickleigh on the way. In fact Bickleigh is just about the only place she would pass through on the main road, a village smaller than Whimple.

Sally's insistence on referring to the River 'Axe' is puzzling. There are two rivers in England so named, one in Somerset rising in the Mendip Hills and entering the Bristol Channel and the other (which surely must be the one 'Sally' knew – if she has the name right) is twenty-one miles long, wends its way through Dorest and Devon, and flows through Axminster and into the English Channel at Seaton Bay. Sally said that her farm was near Whimple which is about seven miles from the River *Exe* in the west, or half as far as the distance to the River *Axe* away to the east; one wonders whether the River Exe was in fact intended after all.

Sally refers to a River Dart and although the source of the Little River Dart is indeed some fifteen miles from Whimple, there is a smaller River Dart that joins the River Exe near Bickleigh (a place Sally has said she knows) and this is probably the River Dart she is referring to.

On the other hand she seems not to remember the River Lowman which although a lesser river than the Exe also flows through Tiverton, in the north-east part of that town; but she did say that she only knew Tiverton "as a place". Nor does she appear to know the River Culm that runs about halfway between Whimple and Tiverton.

It is not perhaps surprising that, primitive and isolated, Sally has no knowledge of Blundell's, the public school for

boys founded at Tiverton in 1604, a school mentioned by one
of its pupils, Richard Doddridge Blackmore (1825–1900) in
his book *Lorna Doone*, published in 1869; and certainly she
would not have heard of Samuel Wesley in 1756 for this
nephew of John Wesley was not born until 1766; but one
might have expected her to have heard of John, the founder of
Methodism, however vaguely – as indeed she apparently had.
John Wesley was born in 1703 and died in 1791 and he
preached all over the country, making a considerable
impression on the poorer classes who were less in touch with
the established church. He is said to have delivered over
40,000 sermons from 1739 when he began open-air preaching
until his death.

The valiant attempt by Leonard Wilder to substantiate
'Sally Fraser' in the vicinity of Tiverton was not successful and
while there may be a dozen reasons why this was so (accepting
for the moment that 'Sally Fraser' was a real person in Devon
two hundred years ago), the fact remains that without any
real evidence of identity, locality or contemporary people,
identifiable facts or checkable incidents, 'Sally Fraser' must be
regarded as an unsatisfactory witness – unless or until more
evidence is forthcoming; and I was delighted when Leonard
Wilder agreed to attempt a further regression to 'Sally Fraser',
after seventeen years, in my presence.

11
The Return of Sally Fraser

Getting to know old friends again after a break of many years should be an interesting experience. It can frequently be a disappointment. So many considerations apply with the passing the years. Is there still a basis for friendship? Is there still a *rapport*? Have similar interests persisted? As I mentioned at the end of my last chapter, I found the Baileys just the same as when I first met them. I think they were pleased to see that I had not lost any of my former enthusiasm for hypnotism.

After seventeen long years the date of Monday 6 May 1974 was decided upon for the 'great leap back into the past'. This time I decided to record a brief introduction to the experiment. As I switched on the tape-recorder I relived that sense of excitement and anticipation that I had felt when many years before Joan had tapped me on the shoulder and said "Switch on your tape-recorder." I decided to ask Peggy a few questions before I hypnotized her and then repeat these questions when she was in deep trance. She should, of course, give me the same answers and might even offer greater information. Hypnotized subjects usually remember more details than when they are in the waking state. In the event of a successful regression to Sally Fraser, I intended to recheck on some of the details she had originally given me and then attempt to get more information about her life on the farm.

Here is the verbatim report of the recording:

"Today is Monday 6th May 1974 and after a gap of seventeen years Peggy Bailey, Bill Bailey, my wife Joan, and myself, but this time in the company of Peter Underwood, have assembled to pick up the threads that we dropped seventeen years ago. I'm sitting next to the couch. Behind me there are Joan, Bill and Peter. On the couch next to me, in the fully awake state is Peggy Bailey. And before we start any form of hypnosis I would like to ask you, Peggy, just one or two questions. First of all, what is your name?"

"Peggy Bailey. Margaret Bailey really, but I'm always called Peggy."

"O.K., Peggy. Are you hypnotized or are you fully awake?"

"I'm fully awake . . . I'm fully awake." (Laughing.)

"Tell me, Peg, have you ever been to Devon?"

"Yes."

"When?"

"I should think about, er, eighteen years ago."

"You've only been once?"

"No, twice . . . twice."

"And how long were you there?"

"A week, about, I think each time, yes, about a week."

"And where did you stay?"

"Er, Honiton. Was it Honiton? Mrs . . . Mrs . . ." (At this point Bill corrected her by saying, "Sidmouth.")

"Sidmouth, Sidmouth." (Confirmed Peggy.)

"Bill said you went to Sidmouth."

"That's right. Yes, it was Sidmouth. In a private house. Yes."

"On both occasions?"

"Yes."

"How far is Sidmouth from Exeter or the Exe Valley? Do you know?"

"Oh, I wouldn't know. Would you?" (Peggy asked Bill.)

"Do you know, Bill?" (I asked Bill. Bill answered this question. "From Exeter, about one hour's motoring, isn't it? Less than the hour.")

"So you would say. . . . Do you know very much about the Exe Valley? Would you know very much about the intimate geography of that part of the country, that part of Devon between Exeter and Tiverton which is quite a few miles north of it?"

"No, because whenever we go I just sit and Bill drives. I never look where we're going." (Laughingly.)

"O.K. Do you happen to know who the King of England was in the year 1760? If you don't, just say so, but if you do, tell me."

"Let me think . . . [a long pause while Peggy thought hard] no, I wouldn't be sure."

"O.K."

"No, I wouldn't be sure."

"All right. There's a very famous school in Tiverton. Do you happen to know its name?"

"In Tiverton?"

"Yes."

"No, I don't, sorry, Leonard." (Bill commented again, "We've never been to Tiverton, have we?" "I think we've passed through, [said Peggy] but I don't know it as a place." "We've never stopped there," observed Bill.)

"O.K. Thanks. Right. [I continued] Do you know the date of the great plague of London?"

"Yes, I do."

"When was it?"

"1665."

"Good. And do you happen to know very much about, er, whether there was any plague in Devon or the nature of any smallpox that might have been there somewhere around the middle of the eighteenth century?"

"Ooh no, I couldn't tell you that, Leonard. No."

"Do you know anything about John Wesley?"

"Well, I was taught at school but I'm afraid it didn't register very much." (Laughing about it.)

"Right. Thank you very much, Peggy. Now Peggy, I'm going to go through the technique of hypnosis [remember, that so far she was in the normal, waking state] and we'll continue from here. Right?"

"Yes."

"Good. Peggy, I'm going to count backwards from ten to one and as I do so, Peggy, you will go to sleep as you have done for me many times in the past. Are you quite comfortable?"

"Yes." (She had been conditioned in her early days of hypnosis to respond to this signal of my counting. Once again I was ready to take the great leap back.)

"Right. Ten, nine, you're getting drowsy, eight, seven, drowsier and drowsier, [Her eyelids flickered and started to close. Her response was rapid and good.] Six, five, eyes closed, four, three, deeper and deeper, two, one, deeply asleep, deeply asleep. [In those few moments Peggy had passed from the waking condition to a state of deep hypnotic trance. It was as though the intervening years had not existed. As though she had been hypnotized by me only a week or two before. It is a well-known fact that a subject will usually respond to the same hypnotist irrespective of a time lapse. Nevertheless, this might have been the rare exception.] Ten, nine, eight, seven, six, five, four, three, two, one, deeply asleep. [She took a deep breath.] Peggy, you will be able to speak to me and converse with me as you have done in the past. At all times you will understand everything that I am saying, irrespective of the age that you happen to be or the date that I give you. But you will always answer me in the language that is appropriate to the situation that prevails when I indicate it and at all times you will understand me."

"Yes." (In a subdued voice.)

"Are you comfortable, Peg?"

"Yes, thank you." (Quietly and so very different from the rather bubbly mood she had been in before being hypnotized.)

"Peggy, you are now in the state of deep hypnotic sleep. You are lying on the couch and I am talking to you. You're quite comfortable?"

"Yes, thank you." (These repeated references to comfort produce a greater degree of relaxation and, consequently, a deeper state of trance.)

"Peggy, I want you to concentrate on your right hand and your right arm as you have done for me in the past. I want you to concentrate on your right hand and your right arm and as you do so you will observe that it starts to feel lighter than the rest of your body and as your right hand feels lighter and lighter than the rest of your body it will start to float up by itself in the air. Feel all the weight going out. It's getting lighter and lighter, lighter and lighter, and it will, by itself, float up into the air. It's getting lighter and lighter. [Her fingers were beginning to twitch quite involuntarily.] That's it, excellent. It's beginning to come. [Her hand was moving up and away from the couch.] Let it come, let it come. It will get so light that now your elbow will leave the couch and float up into the air. [This is a technique for deepening trance and is usually used for sending subjects from light into medium trance. Although from experience I knew that Peggy was already in a deep state, I still went through this routine to demonstrate the phenomenon to Peter Underwood.] You feel well. You feel relaxed and your hand and arm feel delightfully light. It's a lovely sensation and in contrast the rest of your body feels pleasantly heavy and relaxed. The rest of your body feels heavy and relaxed, sinking every moment more deeply into the couch. Your right hand and right arm now are as light as a feather and you can, in fact, forget them for a moment or two. [Her arm and hand were now straight up with the fingers extended towards the ceiling, the entire limb being held at right angles to her body which was lying on the couch.] I'd like you to answer a few questions for me. Have you ever been to Devon?"

"Yes."

"How many times?"

"Twice."

"Where did you stay there, Peg, when you went?"

"Sidmouth. 'Pralines' the house was called, yes . . . no, 'Maylines', that's right, yes."

"Maylines?"

"Yes, Maylines." (She had not been able to give me this information in the waking state as I am sure she would have done. It is noteworthy how the subconscious can be so easily tapped of latent information when the subject is in deep hypnotic trance.)

"Do you know the Exe Valley at all? That part that runs from Exeter up to Tiverton in the north."

"Well, we motored all around but I don't think I could tell you exactly where I was at any specific time. We used to go in the car and just motor around, you see." (It is interesting that she did not know she had answered these questions only a few minutes ago, just before she had been hypnotized.)

"Do you know the name of the King of England in the year 1760?"

(She thought for some time.) "Er . . ."

"It doesn't matter if you don't. You either do or you don't. It doesn't really matter. If you do, you know . . . tell me."

"Is it King? I thought it was a . . . Queen."

"Never mind."

"No, I wouldn't be sure, no."

"Do you know the name of a famous school in Tiverton?"

"A famous school?"

"Yes."

"No."

"Thank you."

"No, I'm sorry."

"Do you know anything about John Wesley?"

"Only that I think he was something to do with the Church."

"Yes, thank you, Peg. Peggy, thank you for answering these questions and now concentrate again on your right hand and your right arm which being lighter than the rest of your body have been up in the air for the last few minutes without any conscious control by yourself. [They had been completely immobile.] As you concentrate on your hand and arm you will notice them getting heavier and heavier and your right hand and right arm will now start to sink gradually back on to the couch. That's right, that's right, it's beginning to sink and as it sinks slowly down you feel yourself going more deeply asleep, more deeply asleep. That's right, relaxing more and more and as your hand and arm fall gently down to your side you feel yourself relaxing. There it is, getting lower and lower, lower and lower and you feel yourself relaxing. Now your hand and arm [here she produced the deep breath which seventeen years before was so significant of a change in her state of trance] are by your side again and your hand and arm now feel pleasantly heavy just like the rest of your body. You feel well. You feel relaxed. [I paused for a moment.] Peggy, I want you to go back in time. [The regression was about to start again. I sensed that the three others in the room shared the same feeling of anticipation that I felt. Peter Underwood had heard so much about the regressions and listened again and again to the tapes. Now he was on the threshold of witnessing it 'live' for himself.] I want you to go back in time and you are getting younger and younger. You're getting younger and younger and you're going back, back in time to your thirteenth birthday. Today, you are thirteen. Back, back, back in time. You're getting younger and younger and you're thirteen. How old are you?"

"I'm thirteen." (Without hesitation. The voice was correct for a thirteen-year-old child.)

"How old?"

"Thirteen."

"And what is your name dear?"

"Peggy Beeching."

"And where do you live?"

"65 Jacksons Lane."

"And do you have any brothers or sisters?"

"Yes."

"Who?"

"John."

"And John is?"

"John's eleven."

"And do you get on well together?"

"Oh yes."

"Jolly good."

"Yes, and Peter."

"Who's Peter?"

"He's my little brother."

"Oh, and how old is Peter?"

"He's three."

"Three?"

"Yes three."

"Right Peggy, I want you to go back in time. I want you to go back in time another ten years. You're getting younger and younger and you are going back now to your third birthday. You will understand me all the time. You will understand me and you are going back to your third birthday. Back, back. Today you are three. How old are you?"

"I'm thwee." (The same response as in the past.)

"How old are you?"

"Thwee."

"And what is your name, dear?"

"Peggy."

"Peggy what?"

"Bee-ching." (Hesitatingly, with the uncertainty of a small child.)

"And where do you live, little girl?"

"In London."

"What part of London, dear? Do you know?"

"Er . . . er . . . Mi . . . tre Street, yes." (With uncertainty.)

"Mitre Street, London. What part of London? Do you know? Are you clever enough to know that?"

"No. London." (She sounded a little irritated.)

"Do you have any brothers or sisters?"

"Yes."

"Tell me."

"Little . . . little bwother." (Proudly.)

"And what's his name?"

"John."

"John?"

"John."

"Good. Thank you, dear. Right. I want you now to go back in time. You will understand me at all times. But I want you to go back in time a long, long, long time. [She took another deep breath.] I want you to go back in time a long, long, long time and if you were somebody living on this earth around about the year 1733 I want you to tell me who you are and all about it. [I had, therefore, conditioned her to telling only the truth. Any regression should, consequently, be dependent upon authenticity. This precaution just had to be taken.] You are going back now to the year 1733 and if, indeed, you are now somebody living on this earth in the year 1733 tell me who you are. [I repeated the condition in an attempt to inhibit any subconscious role-taking. She lay quite still and did not reply for a few moments. Bill's nervous cough is plainly recorded on the tape. Then she started to move her lips in an attempt to speak.] Yes, that's right." (A pause of a few more moments.)

"I'm Sally!"

"You're Sally? Hello, Sally."

"Hello." (Very quietly as though waking from a deep sleep.)

"Sally who?"

"Sally . . . Sally . . ." (Almost as though she were groping through a mist.)

"Take your time. [She took a breath.] That's right. 1733. You said you were Sally. Can you tell me any more?" (I was determined not to feed her with any suggestions but only to encourage her in producing information.)

"I'm seventeen."

"You're seventeen. Good. You're a pretty young girl of seventeen. And where do you live, dear?"

"On a farm." (The Devon burr was well established.)

"And where's the farm, dear?"

"Near Whimple."

"Near Whimple. And where's that?"

"In Devon."

"In Devon, is it? That's a very lovely county."

"Yes."

"Do you have another name as well as Sally?"

"Fraser."

"Sally Fraser, is it? Hello, Sally Fraser."

"Hello."

"I'm very pleased to meet you. [Indeed I was. I had waited seventeen long years for this! Whatever the explanation for this phenomenon, at least she was being consistent. This to me is even more remarkable when one considers that on awakening from her deep trance she has no memory at all of what she has said.] Tell me, do you mind if I ask you a few questions, because I like meeting people and I'm really quite a friendly person. Do you mind answering me?"

"No." (Rather guardedly.)

"Thank you. Er, tell me, do you have any brothers or sisters, Sally Fraser?"

"Yes."

"And what are their names?"

"There's Tom."

"Tom. And, er, is Tom older than you or younger than you?"

"He's older than me."

"I see, and what does he do?"

"He's on the farm, too." (She was answering me in a very subdued voice and completely without any enthusiasm.)

"What kind of a farm is it? Can you tell me?"

"Cows, pigs, grow things."

"What things do you grow?"

"Corn. Churn the butter."

"Oh, you make your own butter, do you?"

"Yes."

"And who milks the cows?"

"I do sometimes."

"And do you have any parents?"

"Yes."

"And where do they live?"

"Why, with me, in the farm." (She sounded surprised that I had not taken this for granted.)

"I see, and is there another farm near you, at all?"

"Not very near, no."

"Where is Whimple? Is it near a big town?"

"No."

"It isn't? Which is your nearest town? Do you know? If I wanted to go shopping, where would I go?"

"Oh, I think Exeter."

"I see. And how would I get there?"

"With the cart."

"With the cart? And who would draw the cart?"

"One of the horses." (Her Devonshire intonation was quite delightful.)

"I see. Do you have many horses?"

"No, two."

"Two. Tell me, where do you keep the animals at night when it's cold, and particularly in the winter?"

"There's a barn."

"Is that near the house?"

"In the yard."

"In the yard. I see. Tell me, you churn your own butter; how about your water, where do you get your water from?"

"To the well."

"And that's near the . . .?"

"In the yard." (She was completely unenthusiastic with her replies. This was possibly because the replies to my questions were really very obvious to her.)

"I see. And how do you get the water out of the well?"

"On a bucket!" (She sounded quite amazed that I should be asking such a question.)

"On a bucket, I see. Can you tell me something about your farmhouse? I don't really know Devon all that well and I find it very interesting. Er, can you tell me something about how many rooms you've got and something about your furniture?"

"Well, the kitchen. The kitchen and [she concentrated] the room off the kitchen."

"Yes?"

"And [she thought again] another room. Father sits in there. And then the stairs from that room and then three rooms upstairs." (She was very careful and deliberate with her description as though visualizing the building as she described it.)

"That's quite a big house."

"No, it's a farm."

"I'm sorry, it's a farm. It sounds a very lovely farmhouse. And what is the name of your farm?"

"Oh, just a farm. Fraser's Farm."

"Fraser's Farm. And do you have any friends? How about any young gentlemen that you may know?"

"Oh, Sam called." (This seemed to please her.)

"Sam calls? Sam who? (I thought she had said "Sam calls", but on listening to the tape I discovered that she had, in fact, said "Sam called". I doubt whether she meant that he had called at the farm just the once. It may have been a local use of the tenses.)

"Sam." (Rather proudly.)

"Does he have a second name?"

"Yes."

"What's his second name?"

"Sam Barnes."

"Tell me about Sam."

"Oh, him very nice."

"Is he? You like him, do you?"

"Yes."

"And where does he live?"

"At another farm."

"Near?"

"Not very. He comes on the cart." (Which confirmed that he had visited her more than once.)

"Do you think perhaps one day you and he may get together and get married? Would you like that?"

"Oh, yes." (Almost confidentially.)

"You would. Tell me, what sort of clothes do you like wearing, Sally?"

"Well, I usually wear my apron, usually."

"You wear your apron. Thank you, Sally. I want you to come forward in time. [She took a deep brath.] I want you to come forward in time a few years and you're getting a little older. I want you to come forward in time to the year 1746 when you are now thirty. [I chose this date carefully. According to the earlier recordings, this was after both her children had been born and before she had lost her parents. It was a tranquil time of her life. I hoped she would be readily forthcoming to my enquiries.] Come forward in time to 1746 when you are now thirty. Sally, you are now thirty. How old are you, Sally?"

"I'm thirty."

"And your name is?"

"Sally Barnes." (Without hesitation.)

"Er, I presume you've married Sam Barnes?"

"Yes."

"And where do you live?"

"On my mother and father's farm."

"And where do your parents live now?"

"With us."

"What all together, or do they have their own part of the house, or how do you manage?"

"Yes, they had father's room."

"They had father's room?"

"Yes."

"And, er, how about your brother?"

"Oh, he's gone to sea."

"He went to sea, did he?"

"Yes."

"How long have you been married, Sally? You are thirty."

"When I was twenty."

"I see. [Her diffidence had disappeared. I can only assume that at seventeen she was a 'shy young maiden' talking cautiously with a strange visitor to Devon. Whether or not she associated me with the interrogator of seventeen years ago I just do not know.] And do you have any children?"

"Yes."

"Can you tell me something about them? I'm very interested."

"They'm twins." (Seventeen years previously it was her grandchildren who had been the twins.)

"I see. What are their names?"

"Tom."

"Tom? I see you named your son after your brother, did you?"

"Well, we called him Tom but he's Terry really." (Without hesitation.)

"I see."

"'Cos Tom went to sea."

"And your daughter's name?" (On listening to the tape, I realized that I should not have said "daughter", as this may have fed her with the idea. I should have phrased the question "And your other child's name?")

"Oh, Mary."

"And, er, how old are they then?"

"They're seven."

"They're about seven."

"Yes, er, yes, they're seven."

"And are they learning to read or write yet?"

"Well, I try to tell them."

"You try to tell them?"

"Yes."

"So they don't go to school or anything like that?"

"No."

"They don't. How do you manage around the house . . . I'm sorry, around the farm? Do you have anybody to help with the washing or housework or do you do it alone? Can you tell me?"

"No. I manage."

"You manage all right?"

"Yes. It's a lot of work." (At last she was beginning to offer a little spontaneous conversation. I felt I had won her confidence.)

"There is?"

"Yes."

"And when it's cold in the evenings and particularly in the winter, what do you burn to keep yourself warm, in the fire?"

"Oh, the trees we cut down."

"You cut them down?"

"Yes."

"And does Sam have anyone to help?"

"Yes."

"Who helps him?"

"Oh, some people come by sometimes on the road."

"But you don't have any regular help?"

"No."

"I see."

"My father helps a little." (It pleased me whenever she offered gratuitous information.)

"You father helps a little?"

"But he's getting old."

"Is he really?"

"Yes."

"And how about your bread, how do you manage about getting bread?"

"Oh, we bake our bread."

"You do?"

"Yes."

"You like doing that, do you?"

"Just another thing to do."

"Tell me, you don't happen to know who the King is, do you?"

"The King?"

"Hm."

"George."

"Which George?"

"Oh, second, I think."

"Thank you very much. That's very helpful. And do you have any pets, any dogs or cats?"

"Oh, lots of cats." (She seemed amused.)

"Any dogs?"

"Yes."

"Can you tell me?"

"A black and white one."

"What's his name?"

"We just say, 'Here dog!'"

"Right-ho. Thank you, Sally. I want you to go forward in time. I want you to go forward in time and you're getting older and older. You're going forward in time another fifteen years. You're going forward in time to the year 1761 and you are now forty-five. Sally Barnes, you are forty-five. How old are you, Sally?"

"I'm forty-five." (Her voice had become comparably older.)

"And how's Sam?"

"Oh, his leg, it hurts." (She had made no reference to this in the earlier recordings.)

"Oh, I'm sorry about that. And your parents?"

"Oh, they'm gone!"

"Oh, I'm sorry. Tell me, were they buried at a local church?"

"Yes."

"Can you tell me the name of the church?"

"St Barnabas."

"St Barnabas?"

"Yes."

"Tell me, if this isn't a personal question, what is your religion? Are you a religious person?"

"No, we just go to church on Sunday, if we can manage."

"I see. And tell me, where is St Barnabas church? Is it in Whimple . . . or . . .?"

"No."

"Where is it?"

"It's just beyond."

"Just beyond Whimple?"

"Yes."

"Thank you, dear. And now that Sam is having trouble with his leg, do you have anyone to help at all around the farm?"

"Yes."

"Who helps?"

"Job . . . Job." (It was Job, whom she had mentioned with such affection seventeen years ago.)

"Just the one man?"

"Yes. He's good."

"He's good, is he?"

"He's good boy." (After all this time she persisted with her sentiments.)

"And where does he live? Where does he spend the nights?"

"In the little place."

"In the little place?"

"The little place, yes."

"What is that, dear?"

"The little wooden place."

"Is that part of the farmhouse?"

"Yes. Beyond the barn."

"Beyond the barn. Tell me, have you had a doctor to see to Sam's leg?"

"No, no. [She sighed.] He send Job." (She was sad at this.)

"He sends Job?"

"Yes."

"Where?"

"To the apothecary."

"And what does the apothecary give him?"

"Some ointment." (She was profoundly sad.)

"I see. Tell me, what happened to your children?"

"Oh, Mary went to service."

"Yes. Where?"

"To Exeter."

"I see. And your son?"

"He ran away!" (She was almost crying as she said this.)

"He ran away? Where to?"

"Yeh. He ran away!" (She was very deeply distressed!)

"Well, don't distress yourself, Sally. Don't distress yourself. All right Sally dear, now. I want you to come forward in time. You're coming forward in time. You're coming forward in time to the present. [The session had lasted half an hour which was as long as I felt a regression should be, without tiring the subject. This was based on earlier experience.] You're coming forward in time to the present and you feel well [she took a very deep breath] and happy and relaxed. You're coming forward to the present time, to the present time and you are now again Peggy Bailey, and Peg, you're lying on the couch and this is Leonard Wilder talking to you. Today is Monday the 6th May, 1974. You're in deep hypnotic sleep. You've had a lovely, lovely rest. [I made no reference, of course, to any regression.] You feel well. You feel relaxed. I'm going to count slowly from one to five, and when I reach five, Peg, you will wake up feeling well, completely normal, pleasantly rested and feeling very refreshed from having had a lovely, lovely, hypnotic sleep and you will look forward to any future sessions, knowing that you will always wake up feeling well and in a good mood. One, two, you're beginning to wake.

Three, four, almost awake. Five, in your own time wake up feeling well. [Her eyelids flickered and she opened her eyes, yawned and stretched. I paused for a few moments.] How do you feel?"

"Ooh, I think I've had a sleep! Ooh! Did I go to sleep?" (laughed Peggy Bailey in her own unmistakable voice!)

The long wait was over. Peggy Bailey had produced Sally Fraser. With one or two minor variations and some additional information, the facts I had asked about where essentially the same as years before. Even her affection for Job had persisted. However, this time it was Sally with a difference. Her former, sunny, outgoing personality did not present itself. Although she softened just a little at the age of thirty, this time she sounded tired, subdued and not particularly forthcoming, which suggested that her life had been a hard and disappointing one. Was this, perhaps, nearer to the truth? Farm life in eighteenth-century Devon could hardly have been easy.

I was relieved when the recording was over. The resumption after seventeen years had made me nervous and tense throughout the session. Not an unnatural reaction, I suppose. Could Sally have 'picked up' these sentiments? Could it have affected her mood? I look forward to Peter Underwood's comments and observations.

12
Assessment and Discussion V

I well remember that day in May 1974 when Leonard Wilder hypnotized Peggy Bailey for the first time in my presence. It was a strange feeling to be present with Peggy Bailey in deep trance and a voice emanating from her in an unfamiliar Devon burr with the apparent personality of 'Sally Fraser' . . .

Before attempting to regress Peggy Bailey on this occasion Leonard thoughtfully (and for my express benefit) went through the whole technique of putting a subject into deep trance although this was not necessary as he could put her under with a snap of his fingers.

To witness such an experiment is fascinating. Whatever hypnosis may be: an artificial trance-sleep; the power of one will to enslave another; total anaesthesia of most of the organs of sense with a considerably heightened suggestibility; or an artificially induced dissociation of the human mind – the process and technique that Leonard Wilder employed left me in no doubt that whatever the origin of the information that came through the prone figure lying immobile on the couch, Peggy Bailey was in a state of deep hypnotic trance.

Hypnotism has a long history and the phenomenon was familiar to the Persian magi, Pagan priests, Indian yogis and fakirs thousands of years ago. The fact that it has long been regarded with awe and associated with magic, mystery and evil probably has its origin in the suppression of hypnotism by the Christian church. Be that as it may, this inherited mental attitude lives on in the distrust that characterizes the reluctance, even today, of many medical and scientific bodies to investigate the undoubted potential of artificially induced sleep with special and important distinguishing qualities.

The emphasis on relaxation which a hypnotist invariably stresses during the course of induction is important from several aspects. The monotonous repetition of the word 'relax' often causes the subject to be hypnotized without knowing it, and without the word 'sleep' even being mentioned. Far more important however is the fact that such a 'relaxing exercise' accustoms the subject to the hypnotist's voice which he or she thereafter associates with relaxation, drowsiness, rest and sleep; and not only that, it also conditions the subject to act on the hypnotist's suggestions. Furthermore when a subject is afterwards asked to describe the feelings and sensations of being hypnotized, just talking about the experience increases their impression on the subject.

Hypnotism causes some kind of change in the function of certain muscles. Usually, but not necessarily, the eye muscles are affected initially; followed by any limb that appears to lose its power when the attention of the subject is directed to it. It is interesting to observe that it is always easier to inhibit a movement than it is to produce a movement. What needs to be known in the field of hypnotic regression is what effect hypnosis has on those parts of the brain concerned with memory and the will to know what is truth and what is fantasy. It was reported in 1920 that a blind subject, under hypnosis, was able to read material put before him. This must surely suggest that the subject, in that particular instance, telepathically received the information from the hypnotist. More research along these lines would be interesting.

Muscular change, as we have seen, is usually observed first of all, in the flickering and finally the closing of the subject's eyes. Often the eyes remain slightly open, but when fully hypnotized the eyeballs are turned upwards, a fact that has been established many times by hypnotists lifting the eyelid of a subject in hypnotic trance. The extent of such muscular change is dependent upon the depth of hypnotic trance which in turn depends upon the strength of the personality of the hypnotist and, sometimes, the method of induction.

These changes in the voluntary muscular system vary from keeping a hand or arm raised to complete rigidity of the whole body (a favourite exercise with stage hypnotists), and it has been established that there is often an increase in strength during hypnosis. One investigator, working with a weak subject who found difficulty in lifting twenty pounds in his normal state, found that the subject, under hypnosis, easily lifted half as much again – and swung it around his head!

It has been suggested that although such experiments point to an actual increase in muscular power, it is indisputable that the strength of the human body is in fact far greater than generally realized and that under hypnosis inhibiting notions and beliefs are removed, releasing the full natural strength for use.

There is no doubt that hypnosis can provoke astonishing physical responses, a fact that has caused doctors in the Western world to look seriously at the witch doctors of Africa and Australia who have used a form of hypnosis for centuries.

In 1974 the *Medical Journal of Australia*, pointing out that within his society the medicine man is highly educated and holds a position of trust and responsibility to society not inferior to European and American doctors, asked whether it is possible for scientific physicians to exploit their position to heal by faith as does the primitive medicine man, and at the same time retain scientific integrity.

If doctors at a research unit attached to the Royal College of General Practitioners in Britain – conscious that medical science is now unlikely to exorcise the witch doctor whose magic is as potent as ever (largely because of his strong psychological hold over his patients) – maintain that witch-doctoring techniques have an important role in orthodox medicine and admit that a form of hypnosis has enabled them to relieve sufferers without drugs, it becomes obvious that the powers of hypnosis are vast and to a great extent unexplored.

There have been many striking examples of the way in which hypnotism can produce hallucinations of the senses and this is not surprising since, although no single theory completely explains hypnotism, it does seem to be established that some form of dissociation of the constituent parts of the human mind takes place.

If we accept that the human mind consists of two parts, the conscious and the subconscious, we can begin to see some of the effects of hypnotism. The conscious mind is that part which is concerned with our daily lives; it is used to plan our work, our home life, our everyday existence. The subconscious mind (which may be subdivided and have various levels) is the complicated organism that runs our bodies without our having to consciously think about it at all. The hypnotist seeks to cause the conscious part of the subject's mind to become inactive and detached so that his suggestions and instructions pass straight through to the subconscious and exert their maximum effect.

It is to the hallucination of the senses that the stage hypnotist owed much of his success, which is well illustrated by the effect he produced by telling a girl volunteer who had been hypnotized that the stage was swarming with mice. She would immediately scream and jump up on to a chair or any other convenient object. Or she would be asked to sniff something pungent such as ammonia, having been told by the hypnotist that it was scent from Paris, and she would say how beautiful it was. Or she would be given a taste of salt and told that it was sugar – or a glass of water and told that it was gin and tonic. In each instance she would respond to the suggestion made to her by the hypnotist and not to what was really there. In the case of alcohol being suggested when water was offered, subjects have produced effects from drinking water which they would normally have produced had they in fact taken alcohol!

The point is that all these hallucinations seem absolutely real to the hypnotized subject, and all the senses can be affected: taste, touch, hearing, smell and sight. Negative hallucinations can also be produced and indeed were produced by Leonard Wilder in my presence. At one point he told the hypnotized Peggy Bailey that I had left the room for a moment and he then awakened her from the hypnotic state and she ignored my presence and obviously could not see me because she had been told that she would not see me at that particular time. The subject – on instruction – is unable to see any person or object, unable to hear sounds or respond to definite scents or tastes.

Converseley hypnosis can heighten the acuteness of the senses to produce hyperaesthesia. Tests have shown that the range of hearing of hypnotized subjects, for example, is sometimes doubled; that the sense of smell is often enhanced, and people have been identified solely by smell – one subject correctly paired a glove with its owner by sniffing it during the course of an experiement with James Braid, the author of *Neurypnology: or the Rationale of Nervous Sleep* (1843).

Other experimentors have noticed an acceleration in their subjects' reactions to sounds and a heightened sense of weight enabling a subject to distinguish one card out of a pack by balancing it on the fingers.

A classic demonstration of heightened visual sense involved the hypnotized subject being shown a pack of blank cards and being told (inaccurately) that one of them was marked in a particular way. After the card was marked by the hypnotist so that it could be identified later, the cards were thoroughly mixed and shuffled and then dealt out. Without hesitation the subject correctly identified the marked card, apparently by noting some slight mark or smudge that was indistinguishable to the hypnotist.

Thousands of hypnotized subjects have 'relived' experiences from their pasts, experiences which they have completely forgotten in their normal, unhypnotized, states; and this procedure has been used with good results in the treatment of psychological disorders, since it enables unwelcome memories that have been repressed to be brought to the surface and dealt with.

Some experimentors feel that this 'age regression' involves something more complicated than merely increased and heightened memory, for 'facts' are often revealed that are unlikely to have been in the conscious memory of the individual concerned. When a subject is regressed to his birthday of only a few years of age, for example, he will not only relate the events of the whole day in great detail but also reveal such details as the day of the week, his health, hobbies and favourite toys, names and descriptions of his friends who came to his birthday party, the reasons for absence of those who were sick or away, his address at the time, his telephone number, the ages of his brothers and sisters, and also such incidental information as the state of the weather, the colour of his new pullover, the number of his father's car, and so on.

The American experimenter and author of books on *Hypnoanalysis* and *Medical Hypnosis*, Lewis R. Wolberg, has maintained that "the consensus at the present time [1952] is that regression actually does produce early behaviour in a way that obviates all possibility of simulation." If age regression of a subject's life is genuine, is the earlier information about previous lives likely to be false?

Since hypnosis can affect the voluntary muscular system, can produce hallucination of the senses, can heighten the acuteness of the senses and revive long-forgotten memories, is it possible that it can release genuine memories of previous lives? That is the big question.

During the course of that first attempt to reach back into the past after seventeen years Leonard Wilder asked Peggy Bailey a number of questions *before* she was hypnotized and the same questions *after* he had hypnotized her and it is significant – as he has pointed out – that information in the subconscious can be obtained very easily when a person is in deep hypnotic trance. Certainly in the case of Peggy Bailey, she revealed information that was not readily forthcoming when she was in her normal waking state. Not much, but a little. Before he hypnotized Peggy Bailey, Leonard Wilder asked her a dozen questions and elicited the facts that she had been to Devon twice, some eighteen years previously (i.e. about a year before the original regression to 'Sally Fraser'); she had stayed at Sidmouth – she agreed when this information was supplied by her husband; and that the date of the Great Plague of London was 1665. She could supply no information about John Wesley; the distance from Sidmouth to Exeter or anything about the Exe Valley; she did not know the King of England in 1760 (George II) or give the name of a famous school at Tiverton (Blundell's), or say whether there had been any plague in Devon in the mid-eighteenth century.

Under hypnosis and apparently in deep hypnotic trance Peggy Bailey seemed to have no knowledge that she had already been asked similar questions when Leonard Wilder repeated seven of the original queries. This time she gave the same answers in all cases except one. She agreed that she had been to Devon twice; she recalled Sidmouth (but did it come from her subconscious or did it appear as a result of her husband's correction when Peggy Bailey was in her normal waking state a few moments earlier?); and – this being the exception – she recalled the name of the house at which they had stayed, saying first *Pralines* and then correcting it to *Maylines*. She still professed to know little about the Exe Valley area; she still did not know who the King was in 1760 and rather wanted to settle for a queen although there was no reigning queen between Anne (1702–1714) and Victoria (1837–1910). It is interesting to notice that 'Sally Fraser' later on during this session had no difficulty in correctly naming King George II. Nor did she know the name of the famous school at Tiverton or anything about John Wesley – except that he was something to do with the Church. It might be thought that if any of this information was in the subconscious mind of Peggy Bailey, rather more of it ought to have come through, and I think I would have been happier if she had been able to add rather more information while in the hypnotized state. On the other hand it had to be remembered that under the hypnotist's influence and in the state of hypnotic trance, the mind can focus on one topic only at a time, there being no extraneous interference. This being so the mind usually operates more clearly and recall is in greater detail under regression than in normal waking life.

It will have been noticed that the first apparent regression to 'Sally Fraser' (seventeen years earlier) followed shortly after the Baileys had in reality visited Devon a year before and inevitably one suspects that this is no coincidence; but what is the connection? Did the visits provide and create a basis for role-taking; or did they perhaps stimulate a deep psychic memory dating back two hundred years to when the area had been familiar in another incarnation?

One of the more interesting aspects of this particular regression concerned the mention by Peggy Bailey, at the apparent age of thirteen, of her brother Peter. This brother had not been mentioned at any previous regression but, since the age difference between the brothers was eight years, Peter had not been born at the time when the subject had previously been questioned about her family. This suggests that she was actually reliving the experience and not merely recalling it from her memory, otherwise at the earlier session she would have been likely to have added, for example, "I had another brother who was born later."

It is noticeable that later in the present regression when she
is apparently three years old, she speaks of having one little
brother (John, two years her junior); Peter, not born for
another seven years, is not mentioned.

Once again certain elements of authenticity are apparent
and these are especially noticeable when Peggy Bailey is
regressed to the age of three (as just mentioned) and having
given her address as Mitre Street, the hypnotist asks the little
child whether she knows what part of London that street
occupies. Exactly as a child of that age would do, Peggy
becomes a little peeved and vexed when pressed to give
information it does not know and out comes: "No, London,"
in an irritable voice. The intonation, pronunciation, hesitation
and vocabularly are certainly those of a young child, and seem
to be completely in character.

It should be noted that the complete lack of enthusiasm and
reluctance to co-operate with the hypnotist at certain times
hardly squares with the theory of role-taking for then the
subject, lost in his or her world of fantasy and make-believe, is
only too ready to supply all sorts of information, much of it
uncheckable and all of it nonsense, but information – of a kind
– does come through, bubbling out of the subject, and there is
a very real effort at co-operation with the hypnotist; a far cry
from the apathy and disinterest apparent during this session.

Another very interesting item came from 'Sally Fraser'
when she was asked where her parents lived and she replied
"With me, on the farm" and she sounded surprised that this
fact had not been taken for granted. Almshouses or at any rate
housing for the "poor and impotent" and those "reduced in
strength as rarely or never to be able to raise themselves
without the assistance of another" were in existence during
the twelfth century; the 'hospital' at St Cross, Winchester, for
example, was founded by the Knights Hospitallers in 1151,
but for centuries old people preferred to live with their families
and spurned such places "built and endowed for the support
of those disabled from work by age or poverty" – apart from
the fact that there were many abuses of the systems, abuses
that necessitated the appointment of charity commissioners to
look into the matter in 1823. So it was common practice for
aged relatives to live with their sons and daughters, exactly as
'Sally' stated.

It was also customary at that period, and later, in rural areas, for the female occupants of a country farm to wear an apron most of the time; as it was to cut down trees on the farm land for fuel; and to obtain assistance on the farm at busy periods from casual passers-by, travelling labourers who journeyed up and down the country working for a time at one place and sleeping rough anywhere they could find and then moving on to somewhere else. It was also common practice at that time for farming people to bake their own bread; draw water from their own well; to obtain ointments for ailments from an apothecary – and for sons of farmers to run away to sea! All of this information is completely in character for the period and quite possibly but perhaps somewhat unlikely to be in the normal knowledge of Peggy Bailey.

There are several parts of this particular regression that suggest something other than role-taking on the part of the hypnotized subject. Would a role-taker, for instance, have insisted on the farmhouse being called a farm and not a house? Or have been so precise about the locality of St Barnabas church: "Is it in Whimple?" ... "No." ... "Where is it?" ... "It's just beyond" ... "Just beyond Whimple?" ... "Yes". Furthermore it will be noticed that 'Sally Fraser' frequently produced a sentiment before the question relating to it had been asked; this might be considered highly unlikely in roletaking.

Occasionally but only very occasionally it is possible to criticize the hypnotist for asking 'feed' questions and for suggesting ideas. There was the idea that Sally might marry Sam one day, and the question when Sally was asked the name of her *daughter*; and yet it could be argued that if Sally had not been prepared to accept 'daughter' she would have corrected Leonard Wilder, as she did a little earlier when he referred to the farm as a house.

A critic might also suggest that Leonard Wilder, when he asked about Sally's children, saying "I'm very interested," could have asked who she thought he, Leonard Wilder, was; but this, he tells me, might have disturbed the state of trance and caused difficulties without really adding anything significant to the experiment.

Equally a critic would pounce on the fact that this time 'Sally Fraser' stated that her own children were twins whereas seventeen years previously she had said it was her grandchildren who were twins; and also the rather odd situation where she said the boy's name was Tom (whereas she had previously said it was Terry), a predicament that was swiftly averted when Leonard Wilder suggested the boy had been named after Sally's brother: "Well, we call him Tom but he's Terry really."

Here perhaps one can begin to glimpse something of the complexity of a situation where the subconscious is apparently tapped and in spite of precautions inserted by the hypnotist, contradictions manifest themselves, causing confusion and doubt. If the subconscious is capable of confusing facts or rather if confusing facts come from the subconscious, may not everything thought to originate in the subconscious be confused, inaccurate and fantasy-orientated? It is a point that must be borne in mind in any evaluation of the case.

On the other hand certain facts were forthcoming *only* after Peggy Bailey was regressed. The reigning monarch for example. Neither in her normal waking state nor when she was hypnotized did Peggy Bailey know who was King in 1760, but when regressed to 'Sally Fraser' she correctly gave George II as the King on the throne in 1746. And as always there was the convincing Devon burr, the little things such as the comments on the cats and dogs about the farm and, just occasionally, local phraseology: "Sam called" and "him very nice" and "Him comes on the cart" and "They'm gone" and "He send Job". If, as Conan Doyle put it in *A Case of Identity*, "the little things are infinitely the most important", then 'Sally Fraser', after seventeen years, returned in triumph.

13
Looking for Liza

Today is Monday 10 June 1974 and today we have arranged for the next session of hypnosis to take place on Tuesday 18 June at 6 p.m. I had no idea how difficult it could be for a number of busy people to arrange to meet on a mutually convenient date. If you have ever tried to organize a dinner party at fairly short notice, albeit for only a few guests, there is always someone who cannot make it. In the case of our 'party' everyone is an essential member of the team. There can be no absentees. Peter Underwood's wife, Joyce, having shown such increasing interest in the development of the investigations, has also been invited to attend the session. She is no newcomer to the subject in general and her comments and observations can only lend weight to her husband's.

The plan this time is for me to put Peggy into a deep trance without the kind of preliminary questions that I asked her last time. I want to start with as blank a slate as possible. I am also, for the first time, going to dispense with the usual 'lead-in' regressions during her present lifetime. Furthermore, I shall take great precautions to inhibit any unconscious role-taking by stating that she will speak only the truth. I can do no more than this. I shall attempt to regress her to the year 1816 in the hope of meeting Liza again at the age of about thirteen. Remember that Peggy has now given us 'Sally Fraser' on a number of occasions. Apart from the very brief first appearance of Liza, this character has only been produced but once and this, of course, all of seventeen years ago. It will be fascinating to see what happens when we plunge so abruptly back into 1816.

Tuesday 18 June 1974, and the team arrived at 6 p.m. It was a warm, sunny day and we were all in good spirits. I felt more relaxed than at the previous session when we had met Sally again. Nevertheless, I was experiencing a sense of anticipation and was, therefore, justifiably anxious to make a start with the hypnosis. I had made a long list of notes which would form the basis of questions that I intended to put to Liza, if and when she was produced. I was going to look for detailed information of her personal life at the Foundlings, while in service with Lord and Lady Frobisher, and later when she was married to Harry Bloggs. I intended to obtain greater details about her living conditions, the district, friends and neighbours, and life in general at that time.

With Joan, Joyce and Peter Underwood, and Bill Bailey seated behind me and Peggy settled on the couch, I switched on the tape-recorder:

"Are you quite comfortable, Peggy?"

"Yes, thank you."

"Good. I'm going to count backwards from ten to one. As I do so, Peggy, you will sink into a state of deep hypnotic sleep as you have done for me before and it will all be very pleasant. Right?"

"Yes."

"Good. Ten, nine, getting drowsy, eight, seven, drowsier and drowsier, six, five, eyes closed, four, three, deeper and deeper, two, one, [a deep breath] deeply asleep, deeply asleep. Ten, nine, eight, seven, six, five, four, three, two, one, deeply asleep. Peggy, you are now in a state of deep hypnotic sleep. You feel comfortable, you feel well, the temperature in the room is just right and the couch is very cosy. All right?"

"Yes, thank you." [The quiet voice of deep trance.]

"You will be able to speak to me and at all times you will be able to understand me, irrespective of the age that you are or the time period in which you find yourself. At all times you will understand me and at all times you will find the experience very pleasaant. [At this point I turned to Peter Underwood.] Peter, would you like to ask her a question?"

"Are you sure you are quite comfortable?" Peter asked her.

There was no reply. I then turned to Joyce Underwood. "Joyce, would you like to ask her . . .?"

"Peggy, you look so happy there," observed Joyce.

This comment produced no response from Peggy Bailey.

"Quite comfy, Peg?" I asked.

"Yes, thank you, Leonard."

"Well, the reason that she didn't answer you, either Peter

or Joyce is, of course, that she is not in *rapport* with you. But she is certainly in *rapport* with me. All right? Good. [By *rapport* is meant that the hypnotized subject can only hear and, consequently, only reply and respond to the person who is conducting the hypnosis.] Peggy, I want you to relax for a few moments and enjoy the pleasant state of hypnosis. As I count backwards again from ten to one you will go very, very deeply asleep, as deep as you have ever been before. Ten, nine, getting drowsier, eight, seven, drowsier and drowsier, six, five, deeper and deeper, four, three, very deep, two, one, deep, deep, deeply asleep. And now Peggy, I want you to go back in time and if, indeed, you were someone living on this earth in the year 1816, you will, when I indicate, tell me who you are. [I chose the year 1816 because in that year Liza, who was born about 1803, would have been thirteen. This is the same age as when I first met her.] But I want you now to go back in time, going back, [a very deep breath] back, back, back in time and if, indeed, you were someone living on this earth in the year 1816, when I indicate it you will tell me who you are, but you will tell me only the truth at all times to the best of your ability. [This should have completely inhibited any unconscious attempt at role-taking.] You will find this all a pleasant experience. Now, you're going back, you're going back, back, back, back. You are going back now to the year 1816. It is now 1816. Now tell me in your own time, who are you? [A deep breath.] Who are you? [With increasing anticipation I waited for the raucous voice of Liza. For a full half minute she lay there quite peacefully but made no indication of replying to my question.] Take your time. [I encouraged her.] It's 1816. 1816. [I waited another twenty seconds.] Do you see anything? Do you feel anything? Take your time . . . Now tell me if you can recollect anything at all . . . Who are you? Now tell me. Now you are free to tell me . . . [I waited another forty seconds. She took another deep breath but made no sign at all that she was going to answer.] Are you going to tell me something? [Where was Liza? At the previous session Sally had been forthcoming so readily. Why not Liza this time? Had my suppression of any role-taking provided that Liza, at least, was just a figment of her latent imagination? If so I would certainly have to apply the same restrictions on the proposed investigations of Lady Alice at the next session; in which case she would not appear were she, too, a creation of role-taking. In those fleeting seconds I marvelled at Peggy Bailey's potential acting ability and I remembered Diana Rigg's comment, 'If this is role-taking then she is a brilliant actress!' Or was there another explanation? Had her psychic memory of Liza been lost in the seventeen years that had elapsed?] Nod your head if you're going to tell me something. [Then to my relief Peggy slowly nodded her head. At last here was the beginning of some communication.] You are? Good. Then I shall be patient. Good. 1816. That's right. Your lips are moving. [I encouraged her. She then lay still again for another half minute.] Are you finding it easy or difficult? [There was no response. Perhaps I should have been more gradual with the regression. Perhaps I should have regressed her a few times as Peggy Bailey before the attempt to 1816. This had always been my previous procedure.] All right, I'm going to make it easier for you. Would you like me to make it easy for you? [She nodded, yes.] Good. I want you to come forward in time now. [A deep breath.] I want you to come forward in time to the present. This will make it easy for you. I want you to come forward in time to the present. Yes, you're nodding your head, yes. That's good. I want you to come forward to the present and today is Tuesday, 18th June, 1974."

"Yes." (Peggy's voice.)

"That's right, Peggy. And you are Peggy Bailey?"

"Yes."

"And you are lying on the couch, being hypnotized by Leonard Wilder and you feel well and you feel happy."

"Yes."

"Do you feel quite comfortable, Peg?"

"Yes, thank you."

"Good. Now Peg, I want you to go back just a little in time. I want you to go back just a little in time and you're getting younger and younger. [The sudden plunge back to 1816 not having worked, I now decided to revert to my normal technique of a gradual regression in my attempt to locate Liza.] You are going back to your twentieth birthday, Peggy. This is your twentieth birthday. Today you are twenty. How old are you, Peggy?"

"Twenty."

"And what is your name?"

"Peggy Beeching."

"And what are you going to do to celebrate your birthday?"

"Well, I can't do very much because of the war, you see."

"I see. How long has the war been on?"

"Since 'thirty-nine."

"Since 'thirty-nine."

"When I was seventeen."

"When you were seventeen?"

"Yes."

"And what are you doing at all? I mean, how do you spend your time? Do you work?"

"Oh yes. I go to work."

"What do you do?"

"At Fords."

"Fords?"

"Yes."

"Do you like it there?"

"Not very much."

"What do you do? What is your job there?"

"I make bearing caps for tractors."

"Well, it's something for the war effort, isn't it?"

"Yes."

"Good. Peggy Beeching, I want you to go back in time. You are going back in time and you're getting younger and younger. You're going back in time fifteen years and today is your fifth birthday. Today is your fifth birthday and it is the year 1926. It is your fifth birthday. 1926. How old are you, dear?"

"I'm five."

"You're five?"

"Yes."

"Are you going to have a birthday party?"

"No."

"Why is that?"

"No. Mummy's busy."

"Mummy's busy? Busy doing what?"

"With John."

"Who's John?"

"My brother."

"And how old is John?" (She thought for a moment.)

"Three . . . I think."

"You are a clever girl."

"Three . . . er . . . yes, yes . . . three."

"Peggy dear, I want you to go back in time and you will understand me at all times. You will always understand me. But you're getting younger and younger and you are, in fact, going back now to the time when you were a little girl of just six months old. You are a little girl of six months old. You are six months old. Hello. Hello. [To the surprise of everyone in the room Peggy hiccuped just like a baby.] Have you got hiccups? [She hiccuped again.] Oh! Mummy? Where's Mummy? Why are you tapping your hand, I wonder? [She hiccuped yet again.] She's got the hiccups. I shall have to bring you out of six months. Right, little girl. You're getting younger and younger, younger and younger. You're getting five months younger. In fact, you are a lovely little baby girl and you are just one month old. You're just one month old. Hello, chk, chk, chk. Hello little girl. [I paused.] Well, she's moving her mouth but there's no sound coming out so we'll regress her even further. Right, little girl, I want you now to go back in time a long, long, time. You are going back in time, [a deep breath] back in time to a time when you were somebody else living on this earth. You are going back, back, back in time and deep down in your memory you will remember, recollect everything that happened. You're going back now, back, back, back to the year 1816. Going back to the year 1816. And if you were someone in 1816, [I repeated the condition] tell me now, who are you?"

A short pause.

"I'm Alice."

"Hello Alice."

"Hello." (The cultured voice of Lady Alice. But what a surprise! This I had not expected! Alice had appeared where Liza should have been. This was just one hundred years before her time. Where was Liza?!)

"Alice what?"

"Alice." (Almost indignant at the question.)

"Well, haven't you got another name other than Alice?"

"Yes, but I don't tell anyone." (I felt like an intruder.)

"You don't? Why is that?"

"Oh, I'm not supposed to."

"You're not supposed to?"

"No."

"Why is that?"

"Well, nurse doesn't like me to."

"Nurse?"

"Yes."

"How old are you, if you have a nurse?" (The notes and questions I had prepared for Liza lay untouched on my lap. Why had Liza not been produced? Could this personality have been forgotten? This was hardly likely when she had been such a colourful character compared with Alice. Unless there was some deep-seated psychic or emotional reason for it. However, here was Alice and it was with Alice that I was in conversation.)

"Well you see I have bad legs."

"Bad legs? How old are you? It's 1816?"

"I'm twelve."

"You're twelve?"

"Yes." (This would have been Alice's approximate age in 1916. I was perplexed by her appearance in the wrong century. Or was this the right century for her? If so, where had Liza come from in the original experiments? I suppressed my frustration and continued.)

"Then you must have been born in 1804."

"Yes."

"What is the trouble with your legs?"

"I can't walk."

"Were you born like this, or has this happened since you were born?"

"Well, I've never walked."

"You've never walked?"

"No."

"Do you have any brothers or sisters?" (It had been my intention to prepare notes on Alice after reinvestigating Liza. I had assumed, in the light of having met Sally again, that Liza would almost certainly be forthcoming. I had been caught unprepared. However, even without notes, I could still remember Alice's life in detail.)

"No."

"You're an only child?"

"Yes."

"And how about your parents?"

"My mother's dead." (There was sadness in her voice.)

"Oh dear, I'm sorry. How old were you when she died?"

"Very small. I don't remember her."

"You don't remember her? And your father?"

"I don't see him very much."

"Why is that?"

"He's very busy." (She was polite but subdued.)

"What does he do?"

"He's in the City."

"And do you know what he does in the City?"

"Lots of stocks and shares and things."

"Where do you live, Alice?"

"In the Square."

"What square please?"

"Portman Square."

"Portman Square? Where's that? What town?"

"London, of course." (She was quite indignant at my 'assumed' lack of information.)

"What address Portman Square?"

"Fifteen." (It will be remembered that previously Alice had claimed to have lived by St James's Park.)

"15 Portman Square, London. Do you have any staff other than your nurse at home?"

"Yes."

"Can you tell me about them?"

"Yes, there's cook."

"There's cook? And what's her name?"

"I just call her cook."

"She doesn't have another name?"

"Yes, but I just call her cook."

"Could you tell me her name?"

"Mrs Smith."

"Mrs Smith. How do you spend your time, Alice? How about your education?"

"I have a governess."

"What's her name?"

"Miss Pritchard."

"And what does Miss Pritchard teach you?"

"The three R's."

"The three R's?"

"Yes."

"Do you like reading?"

"Yes."

"What books do you like reading?"

"Any books."

"Any particular ones that you prefer?"

"I don't mind."

"Alice, I want you to come forward a little in time. I want you to come forward [a deep breath] a little in time and you're getting older and older. You're coming forward in time to the time of your twentieth birthday. So that the date now would be 1824. You're coming forward now to your twentieth birthday and so that the date now would be 1824. How old are you, Alice? [A pause.] How old are you, Alice? [No reply.It will be remembered that in the earlier recording she had died at about twenty-one.] Alice, I want you to go back a little in time. I want you to go back a little in time. I want you to go back to your eighteenth birthday. Alice, you are eighteen. How old are you, Alice? [No reply.] Alice, I want you to go back a little more in time to the time of your sixteenth birthday. You are now sixteen. How old are you, Alice? [No reply.] I want you to go back a little in time. I want you to go back a little in time to the time of your fourteenth birthday. I want you to go back to the time of your fourteenth birthday. How old are you?"

"I'm fourteen." (Then Alice would have died between the ages of fourteen and sixteen. This was a little younger than on the recording made sixteen years before, but was sufficiently correct to act as a confirmation.)

"What is your name?"

"Alice."

"Alice what?"

"Just Alice." (There was this great resistance to giving me her other name, as was the case in the first recording.)

"You have no other name?"

"Yes."

"What is it, please?"

"I don't tell people my other name." (Indignantly.)

"Then what is your father's name?"

"Sinclair." (With indifference.)

"That's his Christian name or his surname?"

"His surname."

"So you're Alice Sinclair, are you?"

"Yes." (She barked the word at me as though to say, "You've insisted so much that here is a name to satisfy you!")

"I'm sorry. [I owed her an apology for my apparently discourteous insistence.] Tell me, how is your health?"

"Not very good. My legs . . . and . . . I get weaker all the time."

"How old are you?"

"I'm thirteen."

"You're thirteen?"

"Yes." (This was incorrect. She had said only a few minutes before that she was fourteen. A deeply entranced subject is remarkably accurate, especially with a very recently made statement. I cannot account for this error.)

"What is the date? What year is it, please?"

"Why do you ask me all these questions?" (She sounded tired and resentful.)

"Well you see, I'm a medical man and I might be able to help you."

"I don't know you." (With suspicion.)

"You don't know me?"

"No."

"Who is your normal doctor? Who comes to see you? We want to help you."

"Doctor James."

"And where does he live?"

"I think Sloane Street."

"Sloane Street?"

"I think."

"Does he specialize in anything?"

"No. But he only comes to see me . . ."

"What does he do for you?"

"He moves my legs."

"And what does he say?"

"Shakes his head."

"What does he say the trouble is? Has he given it a name?"

"He tells father."

"And has your father not told you anything?"

"No. He says I'm getting better."

"Do you agree?"

"I don't feel very strong." (She sounded tired.)

"What treatment are you having?"

"Medicine."

"Do you know what the medicine is?"

"No."

"How often do you have to take it?"

"Twice a day."

"Do you have any friends of your own age who come to visit you at all?"

"No."

"You don't?"

"No."

"So you don't have much contact with the outside world?"

"No."

"Thank you, dear. I want you to come forward in time just a little. I want you to come forward in time just a little to your fifteenth birthday. Can you tell me how old you are? [There was no reply.] Right, dear, you will go back to your twelfth birthday. Alice, this is your twelfth birthday. How are you going to spend it?"

"I shall read."

"What book are you going to read? Have you decided?" (I was interested to see if she would give me a title that had been published in the latter part of the nineteenth century. This would confirm that Alice had turned up a hundred years too soon.)

"There are lots of books, nice books about birds."

"Do you know the names of the authors?"

"Birds. No, I don't bother. No. Birds, nice."

"What birds do you like?"

"All kinds of birds."

"And how are you getting on with your governess?"

"Quite well."

"Good. Can you tell me the name of the reigning monarch?

Who's on the throne at the moment?"

"King George."

"That's quite right. George the what?"

"George III."

"That's quite right. And what method does your father use for transport, for getting about?"

"In the carriage."

"And what makes the carriage go?"

"Why, the horse." (She laughed at my 'stupid' question.)

"Does the horse have a name?"

"Yes."

"What's the horse's name?"

"Major."

"And who is in charge of the carriage? Who drives the carriage?"

"John."

"So John is the . . . ?"

"The ostler."

"Thank you dear. [I was still determined to find Liza. So I decided to make a brief visit to Sally and then to progress her forward to Liza. This method should work.] I want you to go back in time. [A deep breath.] You're going back in time, back, back, back to the time that you were Sally Fraser. [Another deep breath.] Going back to when you were Sally Fraser. You are now Sally Fraser living in Devon. [Yet another deep breath.] Hello, Sally."

"Hello." (An immediate answer in the voice of Sally.)

"How are you today?"

"Very well, thank you." (It was so easy to locate Sally.)

"How old are you, Sally?"

"I'm eighteen." (It is interesting that unless I indicate otherwise, Sally always comes back at about this age.)

"And how do you spend your times?"

"Oh, round the farm." (I do like her delightful Devon burr.)

"Is there lots to do?"

"Yes."

"It's summer today, isn't it?"

"Yes, very hot."

"How are your parents?"

"Oh, they're well, I think."

"What are their names? What are their Christian names?"

"Which one would you like first?" (She was friendly and her mood suggested a better humour than when we had met only a few weeks before.)

"Father."

"Father's Joel."

"Joel?"

"Yes."

"And your mother's name?"

"Is Sally too." (She sounded pleased to be telling me all this.)

"She's Sally too?"

"Yes."

"And do you have any grandparents?"

"I don't know them."

"Why is that?"

"They're not with us."

"Where are they?"

"Well, I don't know?"

"Have you never asked your parents?"

"No." (She seemed surprised at the fact that this question had never occurred to her.)

"Thank you, Sally. I want you to come forward in time. I want you to come forward in time and you are coming forward in time to a time after you died as Sally Barnes. You're coming forward in time [a deep breath] and your psychic memory will travel forward to a time after you died as Sally Barnes, to a time when you became the next person. You will come forward in time to a time when you became the next person after you left Sally Barnes. You are now the next person after Sally. Now tell me, who are you? [There was no response for twenty seconds. Then her mouth moved very slightly.] That's right, it's coming. It will be pleasant. You will find a pleasant period in the lifetime of who you are after Sally. [A number of deep breaths.] Can you tell me something? [No response.] Would you like me to give you a date? [She shook her head.] You wouldn't? You don't want to tell me any more? [A deep breath with no other response.] Come forward in time. Come forward to the year 1840. [A deep breath.] Come forward in time to the year 1840. [I was determined to locate the elusive Liza.] Now, tell me, who are you? [She slowly shook her head again.] You can't? Then just rest for a moment. [I, too, needed a moment to reconsider my plans] I want you to come forward now, forward in time to the present time. I want you to come forward in time to the present time and today it is Tuesday, 18th June, 1974 and you, Peggy Bailey, are lying comfortably on the couch in a state of deep hypnotic trance and this is Leonard Wilder hypnotizing you and talking to you. How are you, Peg?"

"Very well, thank you, Leonard." (As Peggy.)

"Are you enjoying the rest?"

"Yes, thank you."

"Do I have your approval to continue your hypnotism which you are finding so pleasant?"

"Yes."

"Good. Just the right temperature, are you?"

"Yes."

"And the couch is just nice and comfortable?"

"Yes."

"Peggy, I want you to go back in time, [a deep breath] as you have done for me before. You're going back, back, back in time. You're going back in time now a long, long time to when you were somebody else living on this earth. You're going back in time to a time when you were little Liza [a deep breath] living in London. [I was quite determined to locate Liza. That was the whole purpose of this session. After the sixteen-year wait for her, I wasn't going to let her evade me so easily. So far I had not mentioned Liza by name to Peggy, having only given her the date when Liza should have appeared. As this had produced Alice and then nothing, my only chance now was to indicate a more direct and positive return to Liza.] You're going back, back in time and you will remember yourself now as Liza, living in London. Who are you? [A pause of fifteen seconds.] Who are you? [I waited a full minute while she lay quietly and motionless, breathing gently.] Are you Liza? Shake your head, yes or no, if you think you're going to tell me something. [She slowly shook her head, no.] You're not? [She continued to shake her head.] You can't tell me anything? Right-ho then, dear. Come pleasantly and gently forward to the present. Come forward to the present and once again it is Tuesday, 18th June, 1974. [For the time being Liza belonged to the distant past and to that recording made sixteen years before. Why she had refused to speak to me this time, despite all my endeavours, I just do not know.] Peggy Bailey, you are lying on the couch in a state of pleasant hypnotic sleep. You feel comfortable and you feel well. How do you feel, Peg?"

"Very well, thank you, Leonard." (Peggy Bailey's voice in the quiet, unemotional tone she usually used when answering me in deep trance.)

"In a few moments' time I am going to count forward from one to five. When I reach five you will wake up feeling well and relaxed and completely refreshed from having had a very pleasant hypnotic sleep. You will wake up in a good humour, feeling as you always do after a pleasant session of hypnosis. One, two, you're beginning to wake; three, four, almost awake; in your own time, Peg, five, wake up . . . hello!"

"Ooh! Tear in my eye. Hello." (Peggy sat up.)

"How are you?" (I thought it would be of interest to leave the tape machine switched on for another few minutes in order to record Peggy's immediate post-hypnotic reactions.)

"Very well, thank you, Leonard. Fine. Been to sleep again."

"Are you sure?"

"Yes."

"How do you know?"

"Well, I was lying on the . . . yes, I went to sleep . . . ooh, did I go to sleep? Yes, I did. I always have tears when I wake up."

"Even at home?"

"Yes."

"How long do you think you've been asleep?"

". . . I don't know."

"Well, have a guess." (She thought for several minutes.)

"Twenty minutes?"

"That's a very good guess."

"Is it?"

"Mm."

"Have I?"

"Yes."

"Ah!" (And she laughed.)

"You can double that!"

"Eh?" (She was quite surprised.)

"You can double that."

"Oh no!" (Amazed.)

"Forty minutes."

"Oh no!"

"To the second." (This was longer than I would have normally run the session but under the unexpected circumstances I could hardly have curtailed it. Peggy was quite obviously none the worse for it all.)

"No!"

"Tell me, Peggy, what can you remember about going to sleep this afternoon?" (She hesitated, then . . .)

"You counting."

"Yes. What did I say?"

"You said, 'I'm going to count back from ten to one. Ten, nine . . .'" (She closed her eyes and sank slowly down on to the couch again. I made the following observations into the microphone.)

"Having counted from ten to nine, Peggy has put herself into a state of deep trance. And I've got to say this, much to the amusement and amazement of everybody in the room. Bill is trying to stifle his laughter. She is such a good subject."

"Marvellous," agreed Bill.

"So I'm going to bring her round again this time and keep her awake. Peggy, [I addressed her again.] I'm going to count forward from one to five and when I reach five you will wake up feeling well, completely refreshed from your hypnotic sleep. One, two, beginning to wake; three, four, almost awake; five, in your own time, wake up." (Peggy opened her eyes, woke up and smiled.)

"Oh, I've been to sleep again!"

"Do you know why you went to sleep again?"

"No."

"You've no idea?"

"No. I just must have been tired still. Was I tired still?"

"Well, if I were to tell you that you put yourself under . . ."

"Oh no!" (Unbelievingly.)

"Oh yes." (I mocked her.)

"Well don't tell me how. I shall be dropping to sleep all over the place." (This in fact, would not happen. For safety reasons, Peggy had been preconditioned not to go into trance unless she was in the room I used for hypnosis. Once outside this room she would not respond and, consequently, there would be no risk of her "dropping to sleep all over the place".)

"Thank you very much, Peggy."

This little humorous episode is what we needed after the unexpected results of the hypnosis session. Of course I was disappointed at not having found Liza but events had produced a situation that was full of interesting speculations. We had planned to go on to 'Alice' at the next session. This will now have to be replanned. What surprises is that likely to hold in store for us?

14
Assessment and Discussion VI

The hypnosis session on 18th June 1974 was carefully planned and Leonard Wilder, confident that 'Liza' would 'appear' without difficulty when Peggy Bailey was regressed to 1816, asked me to supply him with some questions to ask her.

I was anxious to find out more about the situation of the Foundling's Hospital, where she had been, and particularly some pointer to indicate that she knew where the Hospital was in those days and some of the little-known practices. I wanted precise information about the house in Piccadilly; about Harry's uniform and army life; more about exactly where they lived and the neighbours; and more about 'Doctor Levy'.

After he had conclusively demonstrated that Peggy Bailey was in *rapport* only with him, I settled back for an interesting session, although during the course of his opening remarks I found myself wondering whether Leonard Wilder telling Peggy Bailey when she was in deep trance that she would only speak the truth at all times to the best of her ability would in fact inhibit any unconscious attempt at role-taking: any *conscious* attempt, yes; but surely any unconscious activity would continue unimpeded by such an appeal even if it reached the subconscious area of the brain. Is the subconscious or unconscious mind able to determine what is its own fantasy and what is conscious reality?

The complexity of regression – and especially after an interval of seventeen years – showed itself with a vengeance when in 1816 (apparently) 'Alice' appeared (a hundred years early) instead of 'Liza'! At first I thought that Leonard Wilder's instructions had been misunderstood and that 1916 had been mistaken for 1816 but, obviously considering the same possibility he promptly had Alice agree that she had been born in 1804! Something very strange indeed was happening, or had happened previously.

'Stocks and shares and things': the way that Alice used these terms suggested that she knew something about shares and dealings on the Stock Exchange – although negotiability on a Stock Exchange is not essential with shares. In either of the dates that 'Alice' gave in the two regressions, 1816 or 1916, stocks and shares would be an acceptable and common phraseology for her father to have used and for her to have been familiar with. The Stock Exchange was founded about 1773, the constitution being contained in a Deed of Settlement dated 27 March 1802 (superseded in 1875) and the London Stock Exchange is situated in the triangle formed by Throgmorton Street, Old Broad Street and Bartholomew Lane in the City of London.

In accordance with our plans for dealing with 'Liza', Leonard Wilder now attempted to obtain detailed information about the communicator's home and in particular the precise situation. Originally 'Alice' had said her home was "near St James's Park"; this time I was interested to notice that she gave a completely different address: "Portman Square" she said, plainly and clearly, adding in reply to a further question, number fifteen. I made a hurried note to check on this address, but my enthusiasm was shattered when, immediately after the session, Bill Bailey revealed that he and Peggy had, that day, come to the meeting with us after visiting their osteopath – who lived at 16 Portman Square! This could hardly have been coincidental and in the light of what had already transpired at this session I began to think that, whatever had happened at previous regression sessions with Peggy Bailey, *this* time the material that came through was the result of fantasy – or imagination – or role-taking – or confusion . . . Whatever it was, it was inconsistent, unreliable and unconvincing. At this stage everything pointed to unconscious role-taking: a mixture of fact and fantasy, reality and imagination, telepathy, memory and invention, and if this *was* the verdict on this particular session, could there be a similar explanation for the previous ones, seventeen long years before?

The obvious intermixing of character and situations seemed to continue when, after being asked about the staff at Alice's home, she immediately referred to 'cook' – as had Liza. Even after seventeen years the identical words were used when the hypnotist asked for the cook's name: "I just call her cook."

On the other hand the present regression to 'Alice' did eventually name the cook as 'Mrs Smith'. At the same time Alice also named her governess as 'Miss Pritchard' but she could not be persuaded to name any particular books that she enjoyed reading. Previously, it will be recalled, Alice had named *The Blue Lagoon* and *Alice in Wonderland* as books that she had especially enjoyed. This time she mentioned that she liked books about birds.

Incidentally it might be thought a little surprising that the twelve-year-old and higher-middle class Alice, when asked what Miss Pritchard taught her, replied "the three R's" since reading, writing and arithmetic (regarded humorously as being spelled 'reading, 'riting and 'rithmetic') are regarded as the essential elements of a primary education. Previously she had said that her governess-cum-nurse, named Celia taught her "a little bit of everything": writing, reading, needlework, painting, music . . .

Sixteen years previously (June 1958) an entity calling itself 'Alice Browning' claimed to have been born in 1897 and apparently died about 1918, although there was never any mention of the First World War or anything associated with it during the course of the communications. This time Alice said she was born in 1804 and seems to have died between the ages of fourteen and sixteen and, while making every allowance for the evident fact that she is not a very bright child, there does seem to have been a lot of contradiction and confusion. Within the space of a few moments she gave different ages for herself, and even her father's surname is now given as Sinclair instead of Browning; but perhaps Leonard Wilder's interjection here is justified. It could well be that in view of his repeated questions about her father's name – which for some reason she was reluctant or unable to supply – she did indeed impatiently give a name, any name, to satisfy his curiosity. And it is worth noting that the apparent irritability, suspicion, aloofness and occasional snappiness on her part is quite in character with some people who are incapacitated, who have little contact with the outside world, whose lives are restricted and often dull and monotonous. It is not impossible that Alice was an illegitimate child of her father's – or perhaps he considered it something of a stigma having a paralyzed daughter; whatever the reason she does seem to have been hidden away from society far more than was necessary.

This time Alice gave a different name for her doctor (previously it had been Somers or Summers) saying that she thought 'Doctor James' lived in Sloane Street, a thoroughfare built in 1780 and named after Sir Hans Sloane, the physician and naturalist whose collections of natural history specimens and books and manuscripts formed the nucleus of the British Museum. It has always been favoured as a residential street for fashionable doctors, physicians and specialists.

It should be noted that during the course of this apparent regression Alice correctly named the monarch at the time, 1817 or 1818: George III who reigned from 1760 to 1820.

As he readily admits, the hypnotist was determined to find 'Liza' and with this aim in view he decided to see whether he could find 'Sally Fraser' and then progress to 'Liza'. Could it be that this determination on the part of the hypnotist, coupled with the specific instructions, played a part in the immediate 'appearance' of Sally Fraser? Deep in hypnotic trance, Peggy Bailey was told: "You're going back in time, back, back, back *to the time that you were Sally Fraser. You are now Sally Fraser living in Devon. Hello, Sally.*"

Be that as it may, the familiar Devon dialect and friendly voice of 'Sally Fraser' emanating from the recumbent Peggy Bailey was quite distinct and different in every way from the clipped and precise voice of the cryptic 'Alice'. The quick response to suggestion is demonstrated when Leonard Wilder said: "It's summer today, isn't it?" and immediately 'Sally Fraser' comments: "Yes, very hot." And yet when Leonard Wilder specifically instructed the hypnotized Peggy Bailey to produce 'Liza' (". . . you will remember yourself now as Liza . . .") there was no response!

It almost seemed as though 'Alice' did somehow appear this time about a hundred years early and this would to some extent account for her 'non-appearance' at a date about 1924 since Peggy Bailey, born in 1921, would then be three years old.

The hypnotist is obviously puzzled as to why 'Liza' apparently refused to speak, yet her disappearance can hardly be due to any change in his technique, otherwise 'Alice' would not have been produced, or even 'Sally'; and it does look as though the explanation lies in some intrinsic peculiarity of the 'Liza' incarnation – but what can it be?

Over the years many peculiarities have been encountered in individual cases that might be thought to suggest the possibility of reincarnation. To start with, few authorities agree on the mechanics and regularity of incarnations although most favour the opinion that since the soul itself has no sex there is no bar to reincarnations of either sex for anyone.

I recall Robert Alexander coming to see me at my London club not long ago. An American, born of English and Scottish ancestry, he is an active member of the American Society for Psychical Research and the Spiritual Frontiers Fellowship and a long-standing employee of the State Department of Revenue and Taxation, rendering – as he puts it – unto Caesar the things that are Caesar's. One day Robert Alexander had a spiritual and psychical experience that altered his whole life.

As a boy of five he dreamed the scenes of a former life, in the year 6302 BC, and saw a beautiful girl picking spring flowers. Thirty-three years later he met in person the soul of the girl he had met in the 'dream of soul memory' and he married her. In other dream-memories he has seen the army of Richard the Lionheart passing his house in Southern England and he believes that his father in that incarnation joined the Crusades and was never heard of again.

His subsequent research and experience in the realm of reincarnation has convinced him that "the individual soul is reincarnated on the average every 144 years for a total of 189 times, making a total of 27,216 years, or one cosmic year." He told me that he believed each incarnation to consist of three parts: the self-revelation of past life-time, the living present of today, and the self-revelation of future lives. After 188 lives, the last nine life-times on earth are, according to Robert Alexander, the time when the soul chooses for itself the vocation that pleases it and after those final nine lives the soul "graduates for reincarnation on another planet in the furthermost reaches of the universe." Such convictions are personal and, says the psychical researcher, not open to proof or disproof. "According to thy faith, so be it unto thee."

Peculiarities in this field have been encountered by Wing Commander Harry Drummond who, like Bill Bailey, is a member of the St John Air Wing, the unique emergency medical air delivery service, run entirely by volunteers, that will take a kidney, blood of rare groups, urgently needed drugs and specimens of human material for vital tests, not only all over Britain (at one hypnotic session Bill had just been to Glasgow and back on such a mercy run) but all over the world and, since the service is run on a twenty-four-hour basis, often at dead of night and in atrocious weather.

In a letter dated 18 march 1974, Harry Drummond described two instances of apparent regression – with certain peculiarities. He writes:

A business colleague of mine for over twenty years was an excellent hypnotist and did a lot of work on behalf of doctors in the north-east who sought his help in cases of depression or anxiety and found his ministrations to help considerably in returning convalescent patients to normal health. He was a very conscientious chap and did most of his work in a quiet way; he did not like publicity and avoided it as much as he could, but he and I often had a quiet chat about this gift of his. Of the two cases I mention, one he told me about and the other I witnessed personally.

The first case concerned an office cleaner, a woman of no education and of very poor social background. My friend was asked by her doctor to give her some hypnosis after a serious operation and in one of his sessions induced her to return to a period in her life when she had been in very good health; this with the aim of re-attuning her mind to the concept of well-being after a long period of mental anxiety brought about by her grave illness. During one of these sessions, she began to speak with a different voice and in a language he could not understand. He did not say anything to the woman at the end of the session, but arranged that at the next treatment, he would bring a friend of his, a Professor in Classics at Newcastle University, to be present in case the thing happened again. It did, and the Professor immediately recognized the language as being Classical Greek! This happened without my friend having meant to take the woman back in time any farther than to a period in her childhood when she had been fit and well. The supposition is that she had had a previous existence in which she had not known anything but perfect health and complete happiness, and that her psyche took over and completed to the fullest extent what had been started.

The second instance I saw personally. We had a young chap in our firm at the time who had been ill and came to my friend by arrangement at his flat where I happened to be visiting. In this case, after some preliminary therapeutic hypnosis, he asked the young man to go back in time a hundred years. This was in 1946. It was amazing to see the change that took place. The visitor began to shiver and was obviously in a state of distress. He was asked his name, what year it was, where he was and why he was so upset. I forget the name he gave, but he said that it was the year 1846, he was in the hold of a ship which he named, in the River Thames, his ankles were sore because he was in irons and was about to sail to Australia, having been sentenced to transportation for some crime or other. The funny thing about this was that we got our London Manager to go along to Lloyd's and check the records of shipping movements for the year 1846, and sure enough, that particular ship was logged as having sailed from Deptford for Australia with a cargo of convicts!

While in Edinburgh, in June 1974, I met a friend of Ada Stewart, an individual lady who merits inclusion in any study of reincarnation since she believes that she is the present incarnation of James the Fourth of Scotland.

Some years ago, after she had established herself as a playwright and television writer, Ada J. Stewart became conscious of a mysterious sense of guilt for what she saw as the plight of Scotland. Over a period of years she found herself gradually being taken over by an identity other than her own and she discovered that she *knew* in astonishing and inexplicable detail the whole life, thoughts, and feelings of James Stewart, King of Scots. But I cannot do better than quote from the foreword in her fascinating book *Falcon: The Autobiography of His Grace James the 4, King of Scots* (Peter Davis, 1970):

These memories have lain in my head, either active or dormant, since my birth in March 1929. Those of which I was conscious I had to accept as being present and inexplicable, having failed to trace their origin; the dormant memories came to light more recently. I must stress that at no time was I deliberately searching for knowledge of an earlier existence, for it seemed to me that to have to pass once through this world was adequate punishment for anybody. It took me all of thirty-eight years to discover that my own problem and the Scots defeat on Branxton Moor were one and the same phenomenon. By that time I was so confused with the conflict of trying to reconcile my two identities – one of them still virtually unknown to me – that I lived with the truth apparent for quite some while before I perceived it.

All of this process of discovery will need to be the subject of a further volume. Sufficient here to say that a king's anguish for the nation he led to its slaughter finally proved stronger than all of time's effort to overlay it with the accumulating years' experience of a new lifespan. So great was that anguish, it came ejaculating out of my present subconscious in the form of a total recall of my own death five yards from the English standard upon the field that is today called Flodden. Even my screams, as I relived it, were precisely in tune with those still ringing in my head from 1513.

Ada Stewart is in no doubt about reincarnation for in her normal waking life she *knows* that she is the reincarnation of James, King of Scots; but Peggy Bailey, in common with most of us, has no conscious memory of any previous life.

Don Garrard, the Canadian bass, who has sung at Sadler's Wells hundreds of times, believes that he has found at least seven of his former lives – and always while he has been singing.

The special appeal for him in the music of Mussorgsky is the part of Pimen, a Russian monk in the opera *Boris Godunov*, and so completely does Don Garrard identify himself with that character that he has no doubt that he was a monk in a previous life. Similarly he is convinced that he once lived as a rather cruel Roman centurion; another time as a witty and cutting French courtier; and another time still as a high priest in ancient Egypt. On the subject of the Egyptian incarnation he is reported as saying in April 1973: "When I sing Rumfis, the Egyptian high priest in Verdi's *Aida*, I know that I lived as a high priest in Egypt, about 4,000 years BC."

For some people, proof that they have lived before comes to

them in a different way and I remember Major Wellesley Tudor Pole OBE, a soldier, world traveller and founder of the Big Ben Silent Minute Observance, telling me of such an experience that convinced him of the reality of reincarnation. He was in Egypt, walking towards the ruins of the Temple of Amen Ra at Karnak, when he encountered a procession of priests and strangely clothed figures on foot and in chariots wending their way among the precincts of the ancient temple. He stopped to watch what he could only imagine to be a pageant or perhaps a rehearsal for a film, for he could see no camera crew or any of the paraphernalia of film-making.

After a few moments he walked nearer and found himself unaccountably attracted to a slave boy in the procession. Although the boy had his back to him, Major Tudor Pole noticed the dress of the boy in great detail: the white robe and the loose girdle of a golden-yellow colour. The boy was evidently a lowly slave for he was wearily leading a camel that carried some important personage in rich apparel, almost at the end of the procession.

Major Tudor Pole followed the procession at a distance of perhaps twenty yards and found himself, for no reason that he knew, consciously willing the boy to turn round. At length the boy turned and, with a profound shock, the Major found himself looking into his own face. He told me he never had a similar experience, nor did he want one, for, as he put it: "There is nothing stranger in life than to come face to face with yourself." He could offer no explanation and shortly afterwards the 'vision' or whatever it was disappeared and the ruins were silent and empty; but of the fact that he had seen himself in a previous incarnation Tudor Pole had no doubt whatever.

Another case suggestive of reincarnation with a 'peculiarity' that he only revealed to me afterwards used to be recounted by Sir Cyril Burt and it is in fact one of the earlier and most instructive case-studies in the literature of psychical research.

It concerned a young Geneva business girl, Catherine Elise Muller (1862–1929), known as Mlle Helene Smith, whose mediumship was investigated by Professors Theodor Flournoy, August Lemaitre, Cuendet and others. Her chief 'control' called himself Leopold and he related fascinating stories of previous lives which he and Helene had shared. They finally resolved into three main romances.

In one Helene was Simandini, the daughter of an Arab sheik, who married, after many adventures, Prince Sivrouka of Hindustani and after many years as his favourite wife, she was burned alive on her husband's funeral pyre. During the course of this 'incarnation' Helene spoke Hindustani and wrote words in good Arabic but seemed unable to speak her native tongue. She did, however, display a remarkable knowledge of life on the banks of the Ganges five hundred years ago and much of it, Professor Flournoy discovered, was confirmed, in the main, in an obscure and old history of India which seemed quite unknown to Helene; in fact only two copies of the work existed in Geneva and investigation satisfied the professor that Helene could only have obtained the precise historical information (given by Leopold) through other than normal means.

During another 'reincarnation' Helene seemed to be Marie Antionette and certainly she acted the role of the queen in a very life-like manner. It was noticed that in this life Leopold, in the guise of Cagliostro, knew no Italian and his handwriting showed marked dissimilarities to that of the Italian impostor and charlaton and he did not furnish a single name, date or precise fact, although, on the other hand, he was archaic in his spelling and he knew all about treating maladies in the manner of the period.

The third romance saw Helene welcoming a young man who, in a disembodied state, had visited the planet Mars. The human, animal and plant life was described minutely, night after night, and the characterization was completed by writing in 'Martian' characters and fluent speech in the same language. The characters used in the writing were completely unlike any known characters used anywhere in the world and the language also seemed quite different from any known language. From the translation into French which she kindly furnished for the benefit of Professour Flournoy, he concluded that the Martian language originated in Helene's subconscious, the vowels and consonant sounds being similar to French. The grammar, inflections and construction also appeared to be modelled on the French language. As a work of art Professor Flournoy considered the construction of the 'language' infantile; as a feat of memory he felt that it was prodigious.

The link in all the 'previous' lives of Helene was the 'control' Leopold. Professor Flournoy traced what he called the 'psychogenesis' of Leopold to a fright experienced by Helene when she was ten years old. She had at that time been attacked in the street by a dog. She had been petrified with fright but at the crucial moment she was saved from the terror that threatened to overwhelm her by the sudden appearance, as if by a miracle, of a person dressed in a long brown robe who chased the dog away and then disappeared before she had time to recover herself and thank him. Years later 'Leopold' claimed that this has been his first appearance and subsequently he is reported to have appeared on several occasions when Helene was in danger and accompanied her until the danger was past.

Sir Cyril Burt was always careful to point out, as did Professor Flournoy, that to account for all the information that came through – not so much factual but of early speculations and history – it seems indisputable that the subconscious mind must possess an extraordinary capacity for collecting information from other living minds (both by normal means and also by telepathy), and for constructing "by progressive auto-suggestion" romantic secondary personalities, and he concluded that Helene's dramatic and romantic narratives were "of just that compensatory nature" that "a psychologist might expect in a girl of repressed intellectual interest".

Another puzzling and unsatisfactory case is that of 'Patience Worth'. American-born Mrs John H. Curran had only the benefit of a "desultory education" and that ceased when she was fourteen. In common with many people, in her youth she cherished literary and musical aspirations that came to nothing and she became a typical American middle-class housewife. Soon after she was thirty she tried a ouija board at a party and before long she was sitting at her own board for hours at a time producing a series of novels, poems and witty aphorisms, all seemingly originating from an entity that called itself 'Patience Worth', apparently a previous incarnation of Mrs Curran.

The literary merit of the writing is considerable and *Telka*, an idyllic Middle Ages poem of some 65,000, words is unique in its Anglo-Saxon purity and has been judged superior to similar works of Maeterlinck, while Dr F.C.S. Schiller, the Oxford philosopher, maintained that the work was a "philological miracle". The novels included *The Sorry Tale*, a story set in the time of Christ, and *Hope Trueblood*, a nineteenth-century romance.

Patience Worth claimed to have been a seventeenth-century peasant girl in Dorset who went to America and was there killed by Red Indians. Some of the statements as to the alleged home and environment of 'Patience Worth' have been verified and the detailed knowledge of Jerusalem in the time of Christ, imperial Rome, England in mediaeval times – and particularly descriptions of farm life and the countryside – is indisputably impressive, but a close scrutiny reveals tell-tale errors and the assigning of things to the wrong period . . . and anyway, what would a peasant girl of the seventeenth century know of ancient Rome or, more puzzling still, what could such a girl know about *nineteenth*-century England?

Dr Walter F. Prince, Research Officer of the American Society for Psychical Research, studied the case of 'Patience Worth' at length and concluded: "Either our concept of what we call the subconscious mind must be radically altered so as to include potencies of which we hitherto have no knowledge, or else some cause operating through, but not originating in, the subconscious of Mrs Curran, must be acknowledged." Professor Allison of Manitoba University regarded the case as "the outstanding phenomenon of the age". More recently, however, Dr Donald J. West, a former President of the British Society for Psychical Research, commented: "One can only suppose that during her ordinary reading and conversation and without realising what she was doing Mrs Curran had been noting and storing up every scrap of relevant information that came her way, until finally it came out in the automatic writing . . . Perhaps Patience Worth was the product of years of subconscious rumination."

Do any of these curious cases in the history of psychic research or any of the suggested explanations – help us with a possible solution to the Peggy Bailey regressions under hypnosis? Perhaps the next session will tell us.

15
The Last Regression

"Ten, nine, eight, seven, six, five, four, three, two, one." The light of consciousness faded from Peggy Bailey's eyes as I droned the words and they closed as she sank into a deep hypnotic trance. The date was Monday 29 July 1974.

It was in 1957 that I started my tentative investigations of Peggy Bailey as a hypnosis subject and the voice of Sally Fraser first called to me from the darkness of her unconscious mind. By an interesting coincidence it was in 1957 that the first Sputnik was launched and its tiny bleep called to Earth from the darkness of its orbit. Since then my investigations have developed into the follow-up sessions that were now taking place. So too, in the years since 1957, has that small bleeping artificial satellite developed into all the complex and sophisticated technology of lunar exploration. Mankind's curiosity has instinctively compelled him in his insatiable quest to search for more knowledge about himself and his environment. It was this same instinct, which lives in all of us to a lesser or greater degree, that has led me to search in Peggy Bailey's mind in an attempt to explore its unknown mysteries.

As with Apollo 17, this was to be our last mission in the present series. The final count-down had been made and the subject was now floating peacefully in the vast space of her unconsciousness.

In a last determined attempt I was going to try and locate Liza yet again. In the event of finding her I would question her on the notes I had prepared before the previous session when she had frustrated us by refusing to 'come to life'. I had also compiled a list of questions based on information Peggy had previously given me as Sally, Liza and Alice. I would bring her to the present time as Peggy Bailey and with her in deep trance see how her knowledge of these facts compared with the details she had given me during her 'relived incarnations'. I would then unhypnotize her and ask the same questions of the normal, waking Peggy Bailey. The results should make a fascinating comparison and create much food for thought.

The tape recording takes up the story as I continued:

"And you will sink, Peggy, once again into a state of pleasant deep hypnotic sleep as you have done many times in the past. You are lying on the couch and this is Leonard Wilder, your hypnotist, conducting you yet again through another session of hypnosis. You're comfortable, you're well, you're cosy, you're relaxed and everything is fine. And you will answer me at all times truthfully and honestly to the best of your ability as you have done in the past. Are you comfortable, Peg?"

"Yes, lovely, thank you."

"Peggy, I want you just to concentrate on your right hand and your right arm as you have done in the past and as you do so you will find, because you are hypnotized, that your right hand and your right arm will, as before, get lighter and lighter. All the weight will go out of them and as the weight goes out of your right hand and your right arm, your hand and arm will start to lift up from the couch as they have already started to do. That's right, let them come up into the air. Getting lighter and lighter. As your hand and arm float up, just like that, lighter and lighter, you feel yourself relaxing more and more. [This time I was going to proceed in the classical way that I had established with Peggy in the earlier sessions. Perhaps in this manner I would eventually bring the reluctant Liza to earth.] You feel yourself relaxing more and more. You feel well. You feel relaxed. Your hand and arm are floating up, up, up, up and you are relaxing. You are relaxing. That's fine, Peggy. And now I'm going to induce in you an even deeper state of trance. Your hand and arm now will gradually get heavy and your hand and arm will sink slowly back on to the couch again. And as your hand and arm sink slowly down so you feel yourself going more deeply asleep, more deeply asleep. Hand and arm getting heavier and heavier, sinking slowly down on to the couch and you feel yourself going more deeply asleep, more deeply asleep. Now your hand and arm are back on the couch. Your hand and arm feel normal, like the rest of your body. Peggy, I want you to go back in time and you're getting a little younger and younger, as you have done before. You are going back in time and you are going back now to your sixteenth birthday. You're going back to when you were sixteen. Today, Peggy, you are sixteen. How old are you?"

"Sixteen."

"And what is your name, dear?"

"Peggy."

"Peggy what?"

"Beeching."

"Where do you live?"

"Willow Close."

"Do you go to school?"

"No."

"What do you do?"

"I'm not working at the moment."

"How old were you when you left school?"

"Fourteen."

"And have you been to work since fourteen?"

"Yes."

"What did you do?"

"Well, I had to do just what would come along."

"I see."

"Some jobs lasted a little while, then I had to leave. I went to work on a sewing machine, er, machining dresses and I wasn't there very long and then they had to close down."

"And at the moment you're not working?"

"No, but I'm going to work soon."

"What are you going to do?"

"I'm going to work in a home-made cake shop."

"What's the name of the shop?"

"The Cake Oven."

"And where's that?"

"Corbett's Tye Road, in Upminster."

"Thank you very much indeed. I want you to go back in time a little more and you're getting younger and younger. You're going back in time exactly another ten years. You are going back now to when you were six. [Peggy took a deep breath.] Now you are six. How old are you?"

"I'm six." (The voice of a six-year-old.)

"And what do you do?"

"I go to school." (Even after all these hours of regressing her, I am always amazed at her remarkable change in voice as she becomes younger.)

"What school?"

"Well, we've just moved."

"Have you? Where have you moved from?"

"From London."

"What part of London?"

"Oh . . . ooh . . . er, Lambeth it is, yes."

"You used to live in Lambeth, did you?"

"Yes."

"Can you tell me the address where you used to live in Lambeth?"

"Er, Mitre street."

"Yes."

"Er, 66 Mitre Street."

"And where you live now?"

"I live in Linnet Road."

"Linnet Road?"

"Yes."

"Can you spell it?"

"Er . . . it's like a bird."

"Oh, like a bird?"

"Yes, like a bird. Linnet Road."

"And where's that?"

"In Chadwell Heath."

"Is that Essex?"

"Yes."

"Do you like it?"

"Well, we haven't been there very long but I think so."

"And what school do you go to?"

"Just round the corner. Chitty's Road."

"And do you have any friends?"

"Well, lots of children I play with."

"Would you like to tell me some of their names?"

"Well, I don't know them very much."

"I see. Thank you, Peggy. I want you now to go back in time. I want you to go back in time a long, long time. I want you to go back now in time when, if indeed you were someone living on this earth in the year 1816. If indeed you were

someone living on this earth in the year 1816, then as you have
done before, you will remember and you will tell me who you
are and answer my questions which at all times will be
acceptable and pleasant. Good. You're nodding, yes. Now the
year is 1816 and if you are someone, [a deep breath] tell me
then, who are you and what is your name? It is 1816. [A
pause.] Are you someone?" (A longer pause.)

"Dark!" (She whispered.)

"It's dark?"

"Dark."

"Good. [I encouraged her.] Tell me more." (A pause.)

"Very dark."

"Is it pleasant?"

"Yes."

"Good."

"Soft."

"Soft? Where are you?"

"Nowhere."

"Nowhere. Are you someone?"

"I don't know."

"You don't know? But it's pleasant?"

"Yes."

"Do you want to tell me more? Do you think in a moment
or two you will be able to give me more information? [A long
pause.] Would you like me to go backward or forward in time
so that you can identify yourself? Would you like that?"

"Yes, try." (A faint whisper but co-operatively.)

"Try. Backward or forward in time?"

"Forward."

"Forward in time. Right. Let us come gently and pleasantly
forward in time until you are able to stop at a certain time
when you can identify yourself and tell me who you are. It is
as pleasant as that. [A pause.] That's right. Come gently
forward in time. Your mouth is moving. You're trying to tell
me something. [A long pause.] Can you see anything?"
(Another pause.)

"A room."

"A room? Tell me about the room."

"A very nice room."

"A very nice room. Good. Are you in it? [She nodded her
head.] You are."

"I'm Alice!" (Almost surprised.)

"You're Alice?"

"Alice."

"Hello, Alice."

"Hello." (For the second time in succession Liza had failed to appear and yet once again Alice had been produced. I decided to stay with her for a short while before proceeding with the rest of the plan that had been prepared for this session.)

"Where is the room, Alice?"

"A big house."

"In a big house. And where's the house?" (She hesitated and then came out with this surprising remark.)

"Are you one of my pretend people?" (There was always something unexpected and new each time a recording was made.)

"What exactly do you mean by one of your pretend people?"

"Emma's my pretend people." (She gave the name Emma immediately without any consideration or hesitation.)

"Emma?"

"Emma."

"Tell me about your pretend people."

"We play, Emma and I, when I'm by myself."

"Would you like me to be one of your pretend people?" (This is the first time since these investigations started seventeen years ago that she had asked me who I was. I had often wondered about this but had refrained from asking her lest it disturb her hypnotic state by introducing someone into her past. Now I had become part of Alice's world but as a figment of her imagination. It was interesting but gave me a strange feeling.)

"Well, it's very secret. Very secret. [I felt honoured.] Yes."

"I'm one of your pretend people, am I?"

"Yes."

"Well, if you say so then I'm one of your pretend people. So, I'm one of your secret friends, aren't I?"

"Yes. All right."

"What name are you going to call me?"

"*You* must tell me your name. You must." (This was a dilemma. If I said 'Leonard', would this produce a conflict by

associating Peggy's present with her memory as Alice? Here
was a new situation for me. I decided on a fictitious name.)

"My name is Martin."

"Martin?" (She sounded surprised.)

"Yes. Do you like the name Martin?"

"Yes, I think so." (Not very convincingly.)

"Or [I decided to take a chance after all.]   perhaps you
would rather call me Leonard?"

"Yes."

"You'd rather have Leonard, would you?"

"Yes."

"Well, my name is actually Martin Leonard. [I decided to
play safe by having the two names and therefore avoiding a
contradiction at this crucial moment.] So you can call me
Leonard."

"Yes."

"And how's Emma?" (I now had complete licence to
enquire about my other 'pretend' colleague!)

"Oh, she's just come to see me."

"Has she?!"

"Yes. I'm supposed to be resting, you see."

"Why are you supposed to be resting?"

"Well, I'm not very well."

"Oh dear. How old are you, Alice?"

"I'm eleven."

"Are you?"

"Yes."

"And do you know what the date is? What year is it?"

"It's June."

"Is it June? Yes?"

"Yes."

"June the what?"

"June the eleventh."

"June the eleventh?"

"Yes."

"And what's the year?"

"1883." (Without hesitation.)

"1883?"

"Yes."

"And you said . . . did you say you were resting because you
are not very well?"

"No, I'm not very well."

"Oh dear, what's wrong?"

"My legs."

"Oh, I see. What is your second name, Alice?"

"Ah! We're not going to say." (There has always been this great reluctance to give me her other name. Last time my persistence had irritated her. This time her remark was a little teasing but I sensed a determination not to be forthcoming.)

"We're not going to say?" (I sounded disappointed.)

"We're pretending this afternoon."

"Oh, I see. All right. What else would you like to tell me?" (As she was wanting to pretend I thought I would draw on her imagination.)

"You ask me something."

"I'll ask you something. What other pretend people do you have in your mind?"

"Only Emma."

"And now you have two friends in your mind, don't you, Emma and myself?" (She considered.)

"Leonard." (As though this were a completely new name to her.)

"That's right. Well, I'd like you to do something for me, Alice. I'd like [She took a deep breath even before I had made the request.] you to come forward in time and you're getting older and older. You're coming forward now in time . . . how old did you say you were, eleven?"

"Yes."

"Right. I'd like you to come forward in time for me, ten years. Come forward in time ten years and you're getting older and older. Come forward to the time of your twenty-first birthday, your twenty-first birthday. Today, you, Alice, are twenty-one. Now, tell me, how old are you? [A long pause . . . no reply.] I want you to go back, Alice, a little in time. I want you to go back, Alice, a little in time to the time of your fifteenth birthday. Today, Alice, you are fifteen. How old are you?"

"I'm fifteen."

"How old are you, Alice?"

"Fifteen."

"And how are you?"

"Not . . . very well."

"You're not very well?"

"No."

"Where do you live?"

"Berkeley Square."

"Berkeley Square?"

"Yes."

"What address Berkeley Square?"

"Well, it doesn't really matter about the number."

"It doesn't?"

"No, because we have a little black boy outside." (This was always invariable.)

"A little black boy?"

"Yes, the statue."

"Oh, a statue."

"Yes."

"I see. And, er, who made the statue? Is there a name of the person who made it?"

"Oh, no. It's been there a long, long time."

"I see. Do you have any parents?"

"Yes, a father."

"What is your father's name?"

"Sir Robert Lansdowne."

"Sir Robert Lansdowne?"

"Yes."

"So you'd be, er, Alice Lansdowne, would you?"

"Yes." (I can only describe this reply as with the voice of a young person who is being untruthful.)

"Thank you very much, Alice. Now, dear, I want you to come forward in time. I want you to come forward in time and to return now to the present time. I want you to come forward in time to the present time and you are once again Peggy Bailey and today is Monday, 29th July, 1974 and this is Leonard Wilder talking to you as I have done many times before and you are lying on the couch relaxed and well. How are you feeling, Peg?"

"Very well, thank you, Leonard." (Once again Peggy's own voice but still in trance.)

"Thank you, Peg. I'd like to ask you one or two questions and I'm sure you won't mind answering them to the best of your ability."

"Yes."

"Have you ever heard of a place called Whimple?"

"Yes."

"Do you know where it is?"

"Er, Devon . . . I think . . . er . . . yes."

"Do you know what part of Devon?"

"Er, no. I'm sorry, Leonard, no."

"Are you, er, were you good at history at school?"

"Um, I liked it but I wasn't very good at remembering dates."

"Well, do you know anything about the sort of transport that country people used round about the year 1750? How did they get about?" (She thought hard.)

"Now, let me think back. Oh, horses I should think, yes."

"Yes, but if the family went out, what would they travel in?"

"Er, a carriage."

"A carraige?"

"Yes, a carriage."

"Er, you've heard of bubonic plague and smallpox?"

"Yes, yes."

"Can you tell me just a little bit about them?"

"Er, well in smallpox, er, people came out in horrible spots and when they went away they left a scar on the face. Er, with bubonic plague, I think they had sort of lumps come under their arms and they usually died, I think, from that."

"Do you know whether bubonic plague and smallpox were prevalent all over the country or were they confined to certain areas?"

"I think smallpox was over the country. The bubonic plague was more or less in London."

"Do you think the doctors were any good around the year 1750?" (I avoided the word 'apothecary'.)

"Well, as good as they could be, I suppose."

"Were they doctors then, do you think?"

"Yes, I think they had doctors then. Yes, I think so."

"Thank you."

"And leeches."

"Leeches?"

"Yes."

"That's true. They did use leeches then. Tell me, what do you know about the farm life in England round about 1750? I'm particularly interested at the moment about the mid-eighteenth century. Do you know something about it?"

"Farms?"

"Farm life in general."

"Well, I assume it's much like it is today, really. What kind of farms did you mean, Leonard?"

"West Country farms."

"I suppose they'd have cattle as they do now because they still have a lot of cattle there and grow crops and things, I should think."

"Thank you. Do you know who the King was in the year 1746?"

"Now, just a minute . . ."

"If you don't, it doesn't matter."

". . . 1746? er, er . . . George, I think."

"Which one, do you think?"

"Ah, crumbs!"

"Not to worry."

"Ah, sorry."

"Tell me, does the name Job or Joel have any significance to you?"

"Job? Joel? [In a pensive whisper.] Joel McCree is an actor."

"Good."

". . . was."

"Does the word 'Beauty' as a name mean anything to you?"

"Yes. Black Beauty the horse. I used to like *Black Beauty* when I was at school.

"Now Peg, what are you like at dramatic art?"

"Grammatic art?"

"Dramatic art."

"Um, well, er, I was in a school play and when we were at, er, when I was in my teens I used to go to the hall and we'd do little plays there. I don't think I've ever done anything since."

"If I asked you to impersonate a Devonshire accent, do you think you could do it?"

"I could try. What would you like me to say?"

"What would you like to say? Do you know a nursery

rhyme? How about 'Good King Wenceslas', as though you'd come from Devonshire?"

"Oh, oh, . . . Good King WencLAS-LAS . . . no I'm sorry."

"I think I should have asked you to do a Lancashire one. That was a very good (Lancashire) one. O.K. Do you know anything about Lambeth?"

"Yes. I used to live in Lambeth when I was little."

"Have you ever heard of a place called 'The Cut' or Cutt's Walk?"

"Yes, the Cut, yes, yes. I know where that was but I think it was all bombed away."

"Do you know anything about an illness called angina?"

"Yes, my grandfather died with that."

"Can you tell me just a little bit about it?"

"Er, well, it's heart trouble."

"What happens?"

"I think you just have a seizure and die."

"Do you know anything about the treatment?"

"Treatment?"

"Hm."

"Well, Grandfather didn't have any treatment. They didn't really know he was ill and he just died."

"Have you ever heard of a place called 'The Foundlings'?"

"No, Leonard, I haven't."

"Can you describe the military uniform around the year 1820? I know it's a difficult question. If you can't, say so."

"1820. Can you tell me what times? Is that Victorian times?"

"It would be before Victorian times."

"Before Victorian times. Military uniform?"

"Yes, in this country."

"Well, er, I think, I think it was a red tunic and navy-blue trousers, I think."

"And do they wear a hat? Well, obviously they did. What sort of hat?"

"A round hat, I think."

"Tell me, what doctors' names do you know, doctors that you have met during your lifetime? Can you remember a few names?"

"My own doctors?"

"Yes."

"I'll . . ., yes, yes, I'll try. er, Dr Gose, Dr Stein, Dr Bennett, we knew at the club. [Presumably the Flying Club.] Er, wait a minute, er, er, our doctor's in the village, Dr Gooley. Any more?"

"That's fine."

"That do?"

"Does the surname Bates mean anything to you?"

"Bates? Er . . . do I know anyone named Bates? No, Leonard, I don't know anyone by the name Bates."

"Or the name Bloggs?" (At this she laughed quite suddenly.)

"Bloggs? Ha-ha-ha-ha. No, sorry I don't!"

"Why do you find that funny?"

"Ha-ha-ha-ha-sort of a funny ha-ha-ha-ha name!"

"Do you know—"

"Sorry, ha-ha, Leonard."

"Do you know the name Lever? The name Dr Lever, does that mean anything to you?"

"Lever? No, I only know Lever Bros., the soap people." (She chuckled.)

"How well do you know St James's Park?"

"I know . . . what I know of St James's Park the most is that there is a river with a very nice bridge that goes over and you can stand on the bridge and see the ducks."

"Do you have any favourite books?"

"Er, well I think I could probably name several, Leonard, really. Er, you mean now books or childhood books?"

"Childhood books, sort of early teens."

"I used to read such a lot. One of my favourites was *Alice In Wonderland*."

"Have you ever read a book called *The Blue Lagoon*?"

"Yes, I have, yes."

"Do you happen to know the name of the author?"

"Ooh dear, just a minute, ooh no, sorry, I read the book but I don't remember the author."

"In some part of London, a good fashionable part, there's a statue of a little black boy outside. You don't happen to know where this is, do you?"

"A statue of a little black boy? Little black boy? Sorry, Leonard, no."

"All right, it doesn't matter."

"Lots of statues, but I don't think I know a little black boy."

"Now, I'm going to give you three surnames. I'd like you to tell me if these have any significance for you. Pritchard, Browning, Sinclair." (She thought for a moment.)

"Dad used to know a Mr Pritchard. Robert Browning, you know."

"The poet."

"Yes. And what was the last one, please?"

"Sinclair." (Even in deep trance she was still very much Peggy and able to converse quite naturally. The difference was that her perceptual acuity should be heightened.)

"No, no, I don't know any Sinclairs."

"Have you ever heard of a Dr James or a Dr Somers?"

"No, sorry Leonard, no."

"Have you ever heard of a Lord and Lady Frobisher?"

"Er, the only Frobisher I know, I think, was in Drake's time. In a book I read about Drake once, I think there's a Frobisher there."

"And one final question. Can you tell me who the king or queen was in the year 1816?"

"1816? [She considered.] No, not really, Leonard, not really."

"All right, it doesn't matter. Thank you, Peggy."

"Sorry."

"No, you've done very well, my dear. Peggy, you're nice and relaxed? [She nodded her head.] In a few moments' time I'm going to count forward from one to five. When I reach five, as you have done for me in the past, you will wake up feeling well, relaxed and refreshed from this pleasant session of hypnosis. One, two, beginning to wake, three, four, almost awake, five, in your own time wake up . . . hello, Peggy."

"Hello." (Perkily.)

"How are you?"

"Fine, thank you. Yes, yes fine. I feel better than I did before. Woken up now. (She laughed.) Had a good sleep." (Yawning.)

"Pardon?"

"I've had a good sleep."

"How long have you been asleep?"

"Well, it doesn't seem very long. I haven't my watch, so I can't tell."

"Have a guess."

"Well, I feel all nice as though I've been to sleep for a long time but I can't have been asleep very long because it doesn't seem very long."

"How long do you think?"

"I'll have a guess . . . quarter of an hour."

"Well literally just coming up to half an hour."

"Oh well, that wasn't a bad guess, was it?"

"Not too bad at all. [It is interesting that each time she underestimated the duration of trance.] Peggy, for the sake of the experiment I'd like you to answer a few questions."

"Yes." (As she had no conscious knowledge of having just answered my questions while she was in deep trance, I had to explain my reason for doing this.)

"All right?"

"Yes, yes."

"You'll confirm, of course, that you are completely awake and that you're not hypnotized?"

"No, I'm really awake now, Leonard."

"Well, this I know. I want to ask you a few questions. I've got a few notes here and the significance of this we'll let you know in due course."

"Right."

"Because you've been kept completely in the dark now for seventeen years I think that is a demonstration of infinite patience." (It is a tribute to Bill that at no time has he divulged any of the information recorded on those earlier tapes. Peggy, too, has been remarkably patient. For her, it has all been one complete mystery, as she has had no intimation as to the nature of the investigations except that she was the subject.)

"You can ask Bill about my patience. I've been married to him for twenty-four years!" (A caustic "Thank-you" from Bill.)

"Have you ever heard of a place called Whimple?"

"Yes, I have, Leonard."

"Where is it?"

"In Devon."

"Do you know anything at all, Peggy, about the form of

transport around the mid-eighteenth century, say 1750?"

"It would be carriages, horse and carriages. Wouldn't it? Yes."

"What do you know about the bubonic plague or smallpox around that time."

"Around that time?"

"Yes."

"Well, I think the bubonic plague was practically incurable, I should think. Smallpox, people used to die with as well and it left all marks on your face."

"And do you think they were both widespread all over the country?"

"Yes, I would think so. I've read books and they mention them in, you know, lots of books. Yes, I would think so, Leonard, yes."

"How good do you think the doctors were about that time?"

"Well, I don't think they were very good at all, as far as I can make out, you know, from reading."

"But they were doctors?"

"Oh yes, yes they were, of a sort, yes, of a sort." (No mention of apothecaries.)

"Do you know who the King was in the year 1746? [She thought for a few moments.] Or Queen?"

"One of the Georges." (Unsure.)

"You don't know which?"

"Oh, no, Leonard. Don't ask me to sort that out for you."

"Do you know anything about farm life in England round about 1750?"

"Not farm life more so than, you know, general life, Leonard. Only the things I've read about in books which is, which is general. You know how you read different books about different things. Wouldn't know farm life any more than the other."

"Does the name Job or Joel mean anything to you?"

"Well, Job's in the Bible of course. Er, Joel? Only an actor there is, isn't there? Joel? Joel McCree, an actor, yes."

"Does the name Beauty mean anything to you?"

"Yes, Black Beauty. My Black Beauty, 'cos I like horses."

"You couldn't impersonate a Devonshire accent for me, could you?"

"What can I say?"

"Mary had a little lamb?"

"Mary . . . had . . . a li'l lamb. That's the best I can do,
sorry." (A suggestion of Lancashire.)

"O.K. We'll move quickly on to the next question."

"What else would you like? I can do someone else, if you
like."

"No." I was particularly interested in Devon at this point.

"Do you know Lambeth?"

"Yes, I do. Yes, I do."

"Have you ever heard of a place called 'The Cut' or 'Cutt's
Walk'?"

"It was called the 'New Cut' but I don't think there's much
left there since the war, Leonard, no."

"Can you describe the military uniform in this country
around the year 1820? Sorry to be so precise with the date but
there's a reason for this."

"1820. [Considering.] Let me think. Er, 1820. I think it was
navy blue with a stripe down the trousers, I think, I think.
With some, er, gold buttons, you know, on."

"And on the head?"

"Oh, I would think, er, no, I'm not sure about the hat,
Leonard. No, I'm not sure, no."

"All right. Do you know anything about an illness called
angina and its treatment?"

"Well, I know the illness, because my grandfather died with
that. Yes, and they didn't know he had it, really. He'd never
been ill."

"Do you know anything about the treatment?"

"Well, only I suppose you'd just have to rest and take it
easy because it's a heart trouble, isn't it?"

"Have you ever heard of a place called 'The Foundlings'?"

"Foundlings?"

"Mm."

"No, sorry, Leonard. No, I haven't."

"Does the surname Bates mean anything to you?"

"Yes, H.E. Bates wrote a book. [I'm surprised she hadn't
told me this during her deep trance as Peggy.] Don't ask me
the book. I can't remember the title of it."

"Do you know anyone of the name of Bloggs?"

"Do I know anyone of the name of Bloggs?"

"Does the name Bloggs have any significance for you?"

"No, Leonard, it doesn't." (No laughter this time.)

"Does the name Dr Lever or Levy mean anything to you?"

"Let's have a think. No, Leonard, I don't know any doctors by that name."

"What doctors do you know?"

"Oh, when now? Now? My own doctor? Dr Gooley. Dr Randell, she's a lady. Er, what other doctors do I know? I don't know many doctors, Leonard, because we don't go to the doctors'. We rarely go."

"We were talking about H.E. Bates who wrote a book."

"Yes."

"Do you have any particular favourite books round about the time of your early and mid-teens?"

"Er, ones that I liked reading then, you mean?"

"Yes."

"I used to read a lot, of all people, Zane Grey, you know, the cowboy man. And all the classics. Dickens, all Dickens' books I read. Er, oh, I think I read most things, Leonard."

"Have you ever heard of a book called *The Blue Lagoon*?"

"Yes."

"Do you know the name of the author?" (She hesitated.)

"Oh, I did, but I can't remember."

"Tell me, Peggy, how well do you know St James's Park?"

"I wouldn't say really well. I've been through it, of course, but I don't know it very well. I think if you put me in one corner I wouldn't know it from others."

"There's a part of London where, I'm told, outside a house there's a statue of a little black boy. Have you heard of this?" (She considered the question.)

"No, I haven't, Leonard. No, sorry."

"Tell me, does the surname Pritchard or Browning or Sinclair mean anything to you?"

"Browning, yes, Robert Browning. Sinclair? I've heard of that but I can't think where. And what was the other one?"

"Pritchard."

"Pritchard? Yes, my Dad used to know a Mr Pritchard."

"Do you know of a Dr James or a Dr Somers?"

"Dr James?"

"Do these surnames mean anything to you?"

"No, Leonard. I don't know anybody with that name at all."

"Have you ever heard of a Lord and Lady Frobisher?"

"Recently?"

"Any time." (She thought for a moment.)

"No, no, sorry, not that I could say I do, no."

"Last question coming up."

"Yes."

"Who was the King or Queen of England in 1816?"

"Was it William of Orange?"

"Thank you very much for the answer. Well, thank you very much, Peggy, indeed. We started these experiments seventeen years ago. We have just concluded them. I would like to thank Bill and Peggy Bailey for their excellent co-operation in having entered into all these experiments with the true spirit of investigation. Peggy, you've come along and you remember being hypnotized each time?"

"Yes. I remember you counting or saying I'm going to hypnotize you."

"And then after that there's been a lapse of time while something has happened! And what do you remember about coming round each time?"

"You counting."

"Yes."

"Yes, you counting and then I'm sort of waking up."

"What can you remember of my counting when I wake you up?"

"'Beginning to wake,' you say. 'Three, two, almost awake. Awake!' Yes, yes." (Which, of course, is incorrect!)

"Peggy, thank you very much indeed."

"You're welcome."

16

Assessment and Discussion VII

The final hypnotic session with Peggy Bailey elicited a great deal of valuable information, not least the fact that Peggy Bailey is not able to impersonate a Devon accent consciously!

The fact that she knew (under hypnosis) that there was a military uniform around the year 1820 consisting of "a red tunic and navy-blue trousers" and "a round hat" is interesting in view of 'Liza's' description of her husband's uniform: "a little round 'at, blue trousers and nice red jacket." Then there is the fact that *Alice in Wonderland* was one of Peggy Bailey's favourite books in her childhood: the very book that young 'Alice Browning' said was *her* favourite; and Peggy Bailey had in reality read *The Blue Lagoon*.

Just how much of all this, one repeatedly asks oneself, does originate from the conscious; how much from the subconscious; and how much from – where?

The similarity of the answers that Peggy Bailey gave to almost identical questions, out of and under hypnosis, emphasizes that under hypnosis a subject reveals what is truly in the subconscious mind, suggesting that perhaps there is substance and reason in the Report published by the British Association for the Advancement of Science in August 1974, where it was suggested that the police could usefully use hypnosis to help suspects and witnesses recall consciously forgotten facts.

Under hypnosis, but in the present time and obviously Peggy Bailey, the subject showed a marked difference in her reactions and apparent knowledge. At one point, for instance, she said, "Let me think back"; how very different from anything she had ever said during the regression sessions. And

then there are the occasional, unconscious interjections of
"You know" in Peggy Bailey's conversation, something that
never occurred in any of the regressions.

There were other, more obvious differences too. Asked
about the transport that country people might use about the
year 1750, she replied "a carriage" (i.e. a horse carriage) but
not a "cart" or "gig" as she had said in regression. Again, on
the subject of treatment for angina, Peggy Bailey professed no
knowledge about any treatment, yet 'Liza' knew and she
accurately described the treatment of her day. Similarly Peggy
Bailey seems to know very little of farm life in England about
1750 ". . . wouldn't know farm life . . ." whereas 'Sally' gave a
good and accurate description of her life on a Devon farm in
those days.

The concept of 'Alice's' 'pretend people' is fascinating! Is
this how the various incarnations look upon the hypnotist (if
incarnations they are)? Is this why questions are sometimes
treated flippantly? And why the entity that is contacted seems
to make little attempt to produce concrete facts? If this were
role-taking it presented an ingeniously inventive mind, the
mind of a child shut away from the world; the 'Alice' as
displayed each time she manifested.

This idea of 'pretend people' could account for a lot of the
puzzling aspects in regression experiments, not only those
involving Peggy Bailey but also other explorations on similar
lines that have been conducted over the years and are still
being carried out. It could well be, I feel, perhaps the most
important thing that came out of the whole series of
experimentation with Peggy Bailey.

It may be that the 'pretend people' idea goes some way to
providing an answer to the apparent confusion that is evident
yet again in the material produced where we are faced with
conflicting information. Last time 'Alice' said she was twelve
in 1816, now she says she is eleven in 1833 (roughly midway
between the dates given for 'Alice' in the two previous
meetings with her); and yet another address is given as her
home, although always her home has been given in a
fashionable residential district of London, formerly St James's
Park, then Portman Square, now Berkeley Square. On the
other hand there is also consistent information: the trouble

with her legs; the statue of a little black boy; the fact that her mother is dead and that her father is alive and titled, although there are conflicting statements as to his name; and this time, understandably perhaps, 'Alice' seemed hesitant about accepting the surname of herself as 'Lansdowne' for previously she had given 'Sinclair' and 'Browning'.

Once again the characterization of 'Alice' is complete and exact. In her own life, Peggy Bailey at the age of eleven would have been likely – as would most children – to have said, "We play, Emma and me, when I'm by myself." 'Alice', it will have been noticed, used correct English and said, "We play, Emma *and I*, when I'm by myself." It is in such matters, small and insignificant in themselves, that one comes across incidental pointers to a consciousness other than that of the subject.

The duplication of indirect information also suggests something other than role-taking. We have already considered the possibility that 'Alice' may have been kept somewhat hidden away for one reason or another and it is a fact that a hundred years ago a spastic or incapacitated child was often regarded as something of a stigma to the family concerned and for this reason frequently lived a restricted and confined life, taking little or no part in the social life of the family, rarely meeting people or leaving the house, and altogether producing a situation that encouraged such activities as 'pretend people' to the extent that the child no longer regarded himself or herself as alone and this may have been what caused 'Alice' to use the enigmatic 'we' no less than three times when asked her second name: "Ah! We're not going to say"; "We're not going to say"; and somewhat more revealingly perhaps: "We're pretending this afternoon" – unless this particular 'we' was used to include her new pretend friend, Leonard.

This time, at the beginning of the regression, 1816 seems to have been a period between incarnation, but it is important to remember that in many psychic investigations precise dates, places and names seem to be confused and inaccurate. This is understandable to a degree. If any adult were to be asked to recall something just twenty years previously and they are given a year, would they be *certain* that the incident or experience they were able to remember applied to that particular year? In the case of an outstanding event, perhaps yes, they could be certain, but if nothing of great moment had happened to them that particular year, it could well be difficult and they might easily confuse the year. How much more likely is this to happen in the event of a century and a half – if what comes through under hypnosis is fact?

I was especially interested in the immediate response this time when Leonard Wilder took Peggy Bailey back, in deep hypnotic trance, to 1816 and there was the whispered word: "Dark". Whoever or whatever was speaking found the situation they were in "pleasant" and "soft": were these pre-natal, intra-uterine memories? The contacting entity did not even know whether he or she was someone, nor where 'it' was; only that it was pleasant. And it is surely significant that, when the hypnotist gave the entity the choice of going backward or forward in time, 'it' chose forwards, and emerged as 'Alice', almost surprising itself, it seems! It was one of those moments that make all the times of waiting well worth while and a moment that tends to push aside reason, scientific enquiry and disinterested objectivity and to linger in the memory far longer than hours of other experimentation. Could this *really* be a pre-birth memory? If so, why should not the other entities also have factual bases albeit confused, contradictory and entangled?

One particularly curious aspect of the later sessions is the absence of any 'Liza' entity. No matter what Leonard Wilder did or how he tried, he could not obtain contact with 'Liza', the cheeky, cheerful and friendly cockney. After the last hypnotic session the Baileys revealed that they had been involved in a second car accident a few years ago. 'Liza' had originally come through in 1958, now it was 1974. In the accident Peggy Bailey had badly bumped her head and afterwards had suffered headaches for a time. It has been suggested that this jolt could possibly have affected the memory brain cells and even effaced all recollections of 'Liza'. This is a possibility that has to be considered, but on balance I would think it unlikely; on the other hand it is by no means impossible that the jolt may have blocked the memory of 'Liza' in some way that we do not yet understand. Why, one wonders, did Peggy Bailey, under hypnosis, find the name 'Bloggs' ('Liza's' married name) so funny?

The possibility of unconscious role-taking must always be borne in mind but it has to be admitted that there is little in this last session to give weight to this theory. The response of 'Alice' to the hypnotist's question "What else would you like to tell me?" provoked the response, "You ask me something." Hardly the reaction of a role-taker, and, a little later when asked what other pretend people she had in mind, 'Alice' replied: "Only Emma." This either shows a singular lack of imagination unless her role-taking had reached a remarkable peak of perfection!

So we come to the end of Peggy Bailey's journeys to what may have been lives on earth before she became Peggy Bailey. It has been a long journey, a fascinating journey, in some ways a remarkable experience for all those concerned and, I suspect, an important and worth-while experiment in the possibility of establishing the evidence for reincarnation that can be obtained through hypnotism. Now the time has come for Leonard Wilder and myself to sum up and present our conclusions.

17
Conclusions

From Leonard Wilder

People ask "Is the time and effort spent on space exploration worth it all? What benefits are there from it?" They asked the same questions of the early pioneers of the aeroplane. Has all the time and endeavour spent on our adventure in hypnosis been worth it? We have certainly not come back with all the answers. That it has stimulated thought and interest in this field is undeniable.

During the writing and development of this book the authors have spent many hours debating views with people who have been fascinated by these studies. I myself have been constantly asked, "What are your personal sentiments as the hypnotist? You have spent hours probing the unknown. What, now, are your conclusions? Do you think that this is a valid case for reincarnation . . . or what?"

I was quite determined at the onset to maintain an open mind although, to me, there were two theories which I considered to be good candidates to explain the results that have been obtained. Reincarnation was, perhaps, the most romantic idea. Man dies, his soul survives and is later reborn to gain more experience from a physical existence that will enable the soul to progress in its 'upward flight'. If this philosophy appeals to you then what a delightful ideal it is. Indeed, how can such an ideal fail to appeal? After all, isn't this the fundamental essence of some religions? Could this be so readily demonstrated by hypnosis? And when the subject in deep trance becomes over and over again a 'previous incarnation', has this proved the hypothesis beyond doubt? That the 'lives' of 'Sally', 'Liza' and 'Alice' when heard on the tapes are anything but impressive cannot be denied. Peter Underwood and I have heard them many times over and, as mentioned, we have played them to a wide range of people, each an expert in his own field. One eminent psychiatrist who has listened to the first set of tapes observed, "The subject would appear to be a normal young woman. I am most certainly impressed although I can't really say why."

The other possible explanation for the phenomenon is that of role-taking and very serious consideration must be given to this. The problem lies in the unconscious storing in the mind of vast amounts of information which under the highly suggestible state of deep trance the subject produces as a 'life' when told, "You are someone living before. Who are you? Tell me about it?" During my work on Peggy Bailey I have time and again attempted to inhibit any role-taking by conditioning her to "relive a former incarnation" only if it is quite authentic. How effective these methods have been is open to speculation. With a deep trance subject they should have been effective. The 'lives' were all of the same sex. Was this purely coincidence?

There are so many interesting and frustrating questions that spring to mind. Why was Sally always the most consistently reliable? Why did Liza defy all attempts to be located after her first appearance? Why did Alice prove to be the most inconsistent in both her dates of appearing and her facts? Despite this, her lucky mascot, the statue of the little black boy, was never far from her side. Peggy, when questioned as herself in deep trance, should have verified so many of the facts she gave me when 'reincarnating'. This she failed to do, which tends not to support the role-taking theory. Conversely, a number of pieces of information, albeit given spontaneously at the time, are suspect as having been triggered off by a date or a birthday.

Is it possible that somewhere within us there is a tenuous spiritual memory, a psychic recording, that contributes to make us what we are? Is it possible that the details and events that created this have long since faded and that the deep trance subject in reliving or playing back these memories clothes the emotions in readily available information from within the unconscious mind? Is it possible that a combination of role-taking and reincarnation is the answer or part of the answer? Does it matter that it is John Smith living in London who breaks a leg while on a ski-ing holiday? The same emotional trauma will persist long after the physical healing of his leg, as would be experienced by Pierre Dupont from Paris who suffers a similar accident. Quite possibly it is the deep emotion caused by an event that makes its psychic impression and that the names and dates are of lesser significance. Whether my name is Leonard or Martin, I was still one of Alice's 'pretend people'. The psychic memory of her sad solitude may have identified her 'pretend friend' by the name Emma just for the sake of presentation. It may not matter what your name is or where or when an event occurs. It may be the psychic impression which is of significance.

For me, these investigations have been nothing but fascinating, exciting and, at times, highly entertaining. It could be argued that, perhaps, the techniques employed might have been different or conducted in another way. What experiment is not open to these observations? As I have already stated, deep trance regression is not new. But this has all been my own experience as a hypnotist. Encouraged by my many friends who have found a great interest in this field, I have recorded the results in the hope that they might stimulate further opinions, ideas and hypotheses.

When Man ventured beyond the confines of his atmosphere into the depths of space he took with him many questions. Some of these have been answered. Now, as a result of his experiences, bigger and wider avenues for exploration and philosophy have opened up. When we ventured beyond the confines of Peggy Bailey's conscious mind into the depths of her greater mind we, too, had many questions to ask. Here, too, with only part answers, other roads for investigation, debate and discussion may have opened up.

If the contents of this book have achieved just that, then the writing of it will have been worth while.

From Peter Underwood

After careful study of the subject over a number of years and practical research for many months it seems likely to me, in retrospect, that the information obtained under hypnosis in so-called regressions is a mixture of factual information from the subconscious of the subject, laced with fantasy; and the idea – which originated without any prompting from Peggy Bailey under hypnosis – of 'pretend people' seems to me to hold the key to the final puzzle.

If the subject, in the dream world of hypnotic sleep, conjures up 'pretend people', surely these are the alleged regressions? And if the subject, under hypnosis, can accept that the hypnotist is another 'pretend person', it would appear probable that all Peggy Bailey's characterizations, 'Sally', 'Liza' and 'Alice', have the same origin and in fact no objective reality. But *some* of the information was not known to Peggy Bailey – *as far as we know*. Nor, it would seem, can Peggy Bailey impersonate the Devon accent; but who can say whether or not she could at some time? Would it not be possible for her to recall, under hypnosis, as a mixture of fantasy and reality, as in another life, her visits to Devon when she must have heard the Devon accent? It has been established that Peggy Bailey, like Ruth Simmons in the Bridey Murphy case twenty years ago, is not any kind of adequate actress and yet they both produced staggeringly accurate accents quite foreign to their normal waking lives. Wasn't it Tennyson who said that none of the things worth proving can, in fact, be proved? Five hundred years ago there was no historic proof that America existed nor, to come to more recent times, was there any proof of the existence of the Dead Sea Scrolls until they were found, entirely by chance, by an Arab.

Psychical research is largely concerned with what cannot be measured or weighed and while it may not have established survival after death, it has caused considerable speculation on the possibility that there may be no sharp division between matter and 'spirit', and in recent years a number of natural scientists have begun to realize that purely material explanations are not sufficient.

By the same token, work in the field of hypnosis with a good subject in the hands of a competent hypnotist may well provide incontrovertible evidence for reincarnation. It may not yet have done so but with perseverence further doors will open.

The late philosopher Bertrand Russell believed continuity of memory to be essential for survival of death and since he thought that memory was connected with the living brain, he did not feel memory could survive independent of the brain. Against this argument it might be suggested that living people survive a considerable loss of memory without ceasing to communicate with others, so, since this continuity of memory is not essential for living, why should it be essential for survival of bodily death?

It is interesting to speculate on the possibility that during hypnosis the conscious part of the brain is shut off and the subconscious part is isolated, but when all is said and done very little is known of the mechanics of hypnosis.

Sir Julian Huxley once told me that he was quite satisfied that reincarnation was impossible. Since the personality depends upon a combination of genes and chromosomes and since the possible number of combinations was almost infinite, it was practically impossible for any given personality to be repeated. As I recall I replied to the effect that I was unaware that the advocates of reincarnation had ever suggested that it was the *personality* that was reborn. There are always at least two sides to a question; in the case of reincarnation there are many possibilities.

Does the answer to the riddle of reincarnation lie within Peggy Bailey? Unlike Ada Stewart, Peggy Bailey is quite unconscious of her possible previous incarnations when in her normal waking state and perhaps it is possible to explain everything obtained by Leonard Wilder from Peggy Bailey under hypnosis in terms of information normally acquired and then forgotten, only to reappear in scattered and fragmented particles. It seems quite impossible to prove that this is so; and there is perhaps equal justification for those who prefer to accept that evidence such as that produced in this book suggests, beyond reasonable doubt, that reincarnation is a fact.

Personally both Leonard Wilder and I lean towards the desirability of a lot more evidence, perhaps from or through Peggy Bailey and perhaps through other subjects, before accepting reincarnation as a proven fact. It is the hope of both of us that this book will stimulate interest in this fascinating work, and in the hope that further examples of possible reincarnation will reach us, we rest our case. Although scientists have taken a big step in exploring the endless mysteries of space, we are only just beginning to explore the vast world of the supernormal.

Select Bibliography

Robert Alexander, *A Psychical Experience* (1970).
Morey Bernstein, *The Search for Bridey Murphy* (1956).
George H. Cunningham, *London* (1931).
Theodor Flournoy, *From India to the Planet Mars* (1900)
Christine Hartley, *A Case for Reincarnation* (1972).
Douglas Hunt, *Exploring the Occult* (1964).
William Kent, *An Ecyclopaedia of London* (1951).
Noel Langley, *Edgar Cayce on Reincarnation* (1969).
E. Montizambert, *Unnoticed London* (1929).
Wellesley Tudor Pole, *The Silent Road* (1960).
Walter Franklin Prince, *The Case of Patience Worth* (1927).
A.J. Stewart, *Falcon: The Autobiography of His Grace James the 4, King of Scots* (1970).
Ian Stevenson, *Twenty Cases Suggestive of Reincarnation* (1974).
Paul Tabori and Phyllis Raphael, *Beyond the Senses* (1971).
John Timbs, *Curiosities of London* (1867).
Brian Vesey-FitzGerald, *Winchester* (1953).
Lyall Watson, *Supernature* (1973).
D.J. West, *Psychical Research To-day* (1954).
Werner Wolff, *The Threshold of the Abnormal* (1952).

Index